Testimc

If you are looking for a resource to deepen your experience of God's love, you have found the right book. There is much to like about *Wanting More*. This book breathes new life into John Wesley's standard sermons by realigning them with the seasons of Advent, Christmas, and Epiphany. The abbreviation and modernization of the texts provides insight for a time such as this. Incisive questions that accompany each chapter make this book perfect for small group discussion and discipling. I find this book to be profoundly biblical, pastoral, and spiritually uplifting.

Paul W. Chilcote
Author of *Multiplying Love: A Vision of United Methodist Life Together*

What a quintessentially Wesleyan project. Roberts and Grosskopf offer lively paraphrases of Wesley's sermons, just as Wesley edited and paraphrased writings from his Anglican tradition. Like Wesley, they extend the themes of the paraphrases, offering their own compelling sermons for contemporary life. This is an excellent resource for congregations as an Advent-Epiphany study or for pastors as a treasure trove for preaching. This book brings Wesleyan theology to life for our time, offering "plain truth for plain people."

Rebekah Miles
Perkins School of Theology, Southern Methodist University

Wanting More offers a fresh reading into the timeless sermons of John Wesley, and connects its truths to our journeys through Advent, Christmas, and Epiphany. What this book has achieved is simply beautiful: in reintroducing us to the words of Wesley, we rediscover ourselves in the grand story of God's love, incarnate in Jesus.

Magrey R. deVega
Author of *The Christmas Letters: Celebrating Advent with Those Who Told the Story First*

With this book, Michael Roberts, with Lauren DeLano Grosskopf, provide us with a resource that is both theologically grounded and deeply spiritual. We are invited to be fellow travelers into the Wesleyan way, seeking Christian community, compassion, and joy. This book connects foundational teachings with contemporary wisdom and will be a blessing to its readers.

Bishop Laura Merrill
Arkansas, Oklahoma, and Oklahoma Indian Missionary Conferences of The United Methodist Church

Michael Roberts is an insightful pastor and leader who I deeply appreciate. This work to draw from Wesley's message in order to illuminate the seasons of the church year is a gift to the church.

Adam Hamilton
Pastor and author of *The Message of Jesus*

Whether you are clergy or a lay person, I highly recommend reading this book, *Wanting More*. I so appreciate the way this work has modernized John Wesley's writings in a way that better relates to our 21st Century church. Michael opens the book with: "God's love comes to us on its way to others." That is so true and so Wesleyan. In Wesley's time, his writings were meant to bring about spiritual revival in the church; much in the same way it is needed in our churches today. Wanting More is a great read to deepen our spiritual connections to each other and to God through the writings of John Wesley.

Bishop Robert Farr
Missouri Annual Conference of The United Methodist Church, and author of *Obvious Wisdom: 52 Tips for Effective Ministry*

Rev. Dr. Michael Roberts is a pre-eminent voice in understanding John Wesley and making Wesley come alive for us today. A study like this one is needed in a season of our own church's history when centering down on who we are and who we have always been is so valuable, and what better time to do so than beginning in Advent, when our lives, our faith, our love is born anew. What a joy to celebrate our foundational faith as we celebrate Jesus coming into our lives as well! I am grateful for this study.

Rev. Dr. Michelle J. Morris
Author of *Gospel Discipleship: Four Pathways for Christian Disciples*

Through *Wanting More,* we are taken on a journey through Wesley's Sermons in a way that is relevant for today's world, real in its application, and relatable to our own lives. Leading up to and beyond Christmas, this is the perfect study for those who want to experience Christ in their lives in a new and fresh way.

Jim Polk
Director of Connectional Ministries and Assistant to the Bishop, Arkansas Annual Conference

This book, *Wanting More,* touches all the bases in this home run devotional resource inspired by Wesley's sermons. Essential theological themes are articulated in a clear and easy to understand format. I am excited to use this resource in my local church as a pastor.

Rev. Dr. Ken Krimmel
Ordained Elder in the United Methodist Church and the West Virginia Annual Conference

Perfect for personal growth and communal study, Wanting More will inspire and equip you and your congregation to experience God's love more deeply and share it with the world. The modern re-tellings, devotions, and reflection resources make John Wesley's 18th-century scriptural wisdom accessible and relevant to our world today. This book is filled with expressions of God's love and joy and is a must-read for your church this sacred season.

Blake Bradford
Pastor and co-author of *Mission Possible 3 and Mission Possible for the Small Church*

In *Wanting More,* Michael Roberts accomplishes two tasks at once. First, he gives excellent, easily accessible paraphrases of some of John Wesley's most important sermons. Then he expands on Wesley's thoughts with messages that are helpful for people today. A book like this has been needed for a long time. Wanting More is perfect for an individual's reflection or to study as a group.

David Livingston
Author of *Getting to Good: Moving Toward a Fuller, More Abundant Life Right Now*

This book will take you on a treasure hunt! As a United Methodist, I've recently become passionate about looking back at our spiritual gems in order to move forward. I was delighted to discover that Michael Roberts is, too. Roberts selects and arranges Wesley's best sermons brilliantly, in plain language made thematically relevant for the holidays. As he says about grace in the second chapter: "You do not want to miss this adventure." You truly don't. Read this book.

Rev. Dr. Stephen P. West
Pastor and author of *Something Happens Here: Reclaiming the Distinctiveness of Wesley's Communion Spirituality in Times of Divisiveness*

In *Wanting More,* Michael Roberts offers a timely set of reflections for leaders in the Methodist tradition, many of whom are desperate to renew their sense of purpose and clarify their "why" in the wake of denominational fracturing and a culture of scarcity in many declining congregations. As a practicing pastor, I am so grateful to have this resource to share in my congregation as we answer the call to revival of the Christian witness for this present age.

Katie McKay Simpson
Pastor in the Louisiana Annual Conference

Wanting More

Advent, Christmas and Epiphany

Inspired by the teachings of John Wesley

Market
Square
BOOKS

MICHAEL ROBERTS

WITH LAUREN DELANO GROSSKOPF

Wanting More
Advent, Christmas and Epiphany

©2024 Michael Roberts

books@marketsquarebooks.com
141 N. Martinwood, Suite 2 Knoxville, Tennessee 37923

ISBN: 978-1-950899-87-6

Printed and Bound in the United States of America
Cover Illustration & Book Design ©2024 Market Square Publishing, LLC

Editor: Sheri Carder Hood
Cover Design: Kevin Slimp
Page Design: Carrie Rood

Scripture quotations used with permission from:

Contents

A note about each chapter

With Wesley's sermons arranged to fit within the liturgical year, each chapter contains a paraphrase of one of Wesley's sermons, a devotion on the same theme, and resources for reflection.

INTRODUCTION

Wesley and True Religion

God's love comes to us on its way to others. That's a way to characterize the Methodist movement. This movement was not born out of a theological dispute but out of a desire to know God more fully and bring God's love to a world in great need. The hope was to bring revival within the church and reform to the world outside the walls of the church. It was a movement of optimism, believing that God's salvation is a present reality and that we really can be transformed to reflect the image of God in the world.

John Wesley was the inspired leader of this early Methodist movement. His organizational guidance and practical theology helped this movement grow. To provide training for the many involved, Wesley gave sermons to teach the basics of faith. In time, several of these sermons were designated as "The Standard Sermons" and became part of the doctrine for the people called Methodists. We are supposed to teach them, yet we have strayed from doing so. After committing to rereading these sermons and finding a wealth of inspiration, I began to wonder why this neglect happened. What factors contributed to our lack of engagement with these sermons?

I suspect that a big reason is their length and style. They

are written in 18th-century English and are very long by contemporary standards. To make them more accessible, I resolved to paraphrase each sermon in fifteen hundred words or less. The hope was to capture the key themes without taking away the inspiration.

This exercise revealed another reason for our lack of engagement with these sermons. In their original configuration, these sermons do not fit into the rhythms of the church year. They do not follow a liturgical pattern or fit naturally into church seasons. For example, there is no straightforward sermon for Christmas, Easter, Pentecost, or for the seasons around these high and holy days. Most often, Wesley was the guest preacher or was preaching outside of a parish context, even as he encouraged all Methodists to be active in their local parishes. This reality sparked the question: Could these sermons be rearranged in a way to align them to contemporary rhythms within the church? In other words, could they be organized to fit the seasons of the liturgical year? Could they be offered in a way that is consistent with other teaching resources within the church today? After reading these sermons and outlining the key theological themes, this possibility began to take shape.[1]

The next step was to develop a system to help individuals, classes, and groups engage in these sermons and discover their blessings. As a pastoral team, we started by sharing one of these paraphrased sermons each week on a dedicated web page. Then we used the themes of that sermon as inspiration for worship and preaching within our own context. The next step was to provide resources for devotion and discipling.

Within this book there are two series – one for Advent and Christmas entitled "Wanting More" and another for Epiphany entitled "More Than." In the first series we start with Wesley's sermon "The Means of Grace." Wesley described these means as resources to help us wait upon the Lord and to open our hearts to all that God wants for us. These means help us to prepare the way. In the second series, we use the first eight sermons in the Standard Sermons as a way to start the New Year. In the first endnote, there is an outline for how Wesley's sermons were rearranged to be used to fit the seasons of the church year. With this rearranging, the hope is to bring these important teachings to life in a new way.[2]

The strongest motivation to move forward with this project was the belief that these sermons continue to have great relevance. They continue to open up the scriptures and give insights into faithful, fruitful living. John Wesley's sermons continue to have the power to bring renewal to congregations. Through this process, we became more and more convicted that these sermons should continue to serve as instruments of the blessings that God wants for us today.

In going through these sermons, we noticed the phrase "true religion" over and over again. It struck us as a provocative and bold claim, especially in an age of diverse theological thought. As Wesley defines it, true religion does not exist within any ritual, creed, or anything "external to the heart"; it is found in love, peace, and joy through the Holy Spirit. True religion is never a claim of power over and against others and is never used to justify division and harm. Such manifestations point to false religion and the reality of evil itself. True religion is illuminated by faith

3

that always works for love.[3] On our pilgrimage through this life, we are called to continuous self-examination as we open ourselves to God's transforming work within us.[4] That is what God wants for us and is at the heart of what Wesley calls "true religion."

In promoting "true religion," it is worth noting that Wesley did not write a systematic theology. His offerings come as direct resources to help people grow in a faith that works for love: sermons, letters, prayers, and hymns. In these resources, Wesley wanted to illuminate "the way of salvation" for us to follow.[5] As a primary motivation, he wanted those who saw religion as mere formality or only in terms of outward practices to know an experiential, scriptural, personal, and heart-transforming faith.

But Wesley did not stop there. He also challenges those who know this "religion of the heart" to understand that it is much more. He calls all to a faith that works for love and grows in love by attending to the outward means of grace that God has given. As we see repeatedly in these sermons, faith is more than believing and more than a heartfelt experience. We are called to a holistic faith that can truly transform us into the image of Christ for the world. These sermons were given for all in search of something more than a one-dimensional faith. Wesley consistently provides us with a "both/and" perspective, joining grace and holiness, experience and action, head and heart, faith and good works, all through an evangelistic message with a call to social engagement. May this spirit shine through this journey.

As another dynamic, Wesley took the "glad tidings of salvation" outside the walls of the church and strived to communicate the ways that would be relevant and meaningful to those beyond the hallowed walls. In his words, he "consented to be more vile."[6] This was a big decision, and it transformed the movement—or, we might say, it sparked the movement. This spirit motivated this book.

Through several revisions, there came to be forty-four Standard Sermons, but many others were published as teaching resources, and some have been considered within The Standard Sermons at times, even by Wesley himself. Several of these additional sermons have been used. Some are historical favorites with great insights into the understanding and practice of faith, even as they also reveal change and growth in Wesley's own theological thought. In seeking true religion, we must be "patient with contradictions," as Wesley says. As we practice this faith, we learn to love in the midst of a blessed diversity of gifts, circumstances, and perspectives. These resources are given to help us learn, grow, change, and, most importantly, love as we worship a God big enough to work through it all.

And now I want to share some important words of thanksgiving, acknowledging some of the deeper roots that led to the development of this project. At both Duke Divinity School where I received an M.Div. and Perkins School of Theology (SMU) where I received a D.Min., I have been shaped as a Wesleyan by many great scholars. I am grateful for the many opportunities I have had to lead workshops on the United Methodist Way and to teach our history and doctrine through Course of Study and Licensing School.[7] Most recently, I am also thankful for the opportunity to participate in a Wesley pilgrimage. It was life-changing. Beloved theological concepts became three-dimensional when envisioning them in the context of time, place, politics, and the consequences of following where the Spirit leads. I pray this series will help bring these inspired theological themes to life for others in the way they have for so many before us.

This book was a part of a yearlong worship and discipleship focus developed within First United Methodist Church, Conway, Arkansas. Reverend Lauren DeLano was one year out of Boston University School of Theology and in her first appointment as the associate pastor when I proposed the idea for this project and invited her to share in its development. Her shared love for Wesley and inspired gifts of ministry brought much energy to this project. She collaborated with sermon ideas, preached her own sermons built upon this collaboration, and helped develop the resources used for reflection and study. Over the course of the year, Reverend DeLano became a valued partner and helped make this project possible. She also participated in a Wesley pilgrimage and experienced how Wesley's thoughts came to life by placing them in the context of time and place. By "conferencing" with many, we have experienced over and over again that which Wesley advocated for all: holy conversation with others that leads to greater insight and inspiration. We are not meant to lead alone.

We invite you into this special journey through Wesley's sermons and pray it will be life-giving for you. As you take this journey, may love grow—first in your heart and then through you into the world.

Michael Roberts

Wanting More

The Season of Advent and Christmas

CHAPTER ONE

"The Means of Grace"
(A devotional paraphrase)

Sermon 16 in The Standard Sermons of John Wesley

"Return to me, and I will return to you," says the Lord of hosts. But you say, "How shall we return?"

Malachi 3:7 (NRSV)

Paraphrase of Wesley sermon

Are there still ordinances to be followed since life has come to light by the gospel? Are there any means ordained by God to be used as channels of God's grace? The answer is "Yes!" In the scriptures, we see many examples of such means or channels. In Acts, for example, we read that the disciples continued in the Apostles' teachings, in the breaking of bread, and in prayers—all important means of grace (Acts 2:42-44).

But there is a danger. Over time, we can mistake the *means* for the *end*. In every age, there are people who see religion in terms of outward works rather than as the renewing of one's heart in God's image. We often forget that every commandment's end, or purpose, is love and, conversely, to purify us from all pride, anger, greed, and evil desires. When we forget this, these God-ordained means can become a source of our own failing.

We must heed this cautionary word. Any show of outward religion is worthless without the religion of the heart. All outward ordinances benefit us only when they advance inward holiness. At the same time, claiming that the means have no place at all is a fatal mistake. This notion can spread so easily. With a new desire to grow in the Spirit, it is easy to become impatient with the ordinary ways of the church as we look for more extraordinary signs. Many have tried the outward means of worship and sacrament, of prayer and searching the scriptures, and found more struggle than comfort, more challenge than bliss. They are easily tempted to cast aside the painful strife of faith for promises of a more direct witness of the Spirit.

So, the question remains, "Are there God-given means of grace?" and "What value do they have?" For a definition, "means of grace" can be understood as "outward signs, words, or actions, ordained by God, to be the ordinary channels whereby God might convey to us, preventing, justifying, or sanctifying grace." To name these means, we start with prayer, then add the reading and hearing of scripture, and then the Lord's Supper. These are examples of the ordinary channels through which God conveys grace.

As we explore these means, we fully acknowledge that they are not ends in themselves. There is no intrinsic power in the letters of scripture, the words of great prayers, or even in the bread and cup. That power belongs to God. Just going through the motions of religion is not enough. We are not restored to the image of God by any works that we do but only by the free grace of God. So, we ask, how shall we practice the faith? One might answer, "By waiting on the Lord." And then the question becomes, "How shall we wait?" God has not left us without direction. We wait in the means that God has ordained.

First, we wait in prayer. In one of many passages, the Lord himself invites us to ask, seek, and knock (Matt 7:7). We hear Jesus say that if we know how to give good gifts to our children, how much more will our heavenly father give the Holy Spirit to those who ask (Matt 7:11)? Our Lord invites us into this blessing by using the means of prayer.

Secondly, we wait by searching the scriptures. Our Lord used this phrase, saying that the scriptures testify to him (John 5:39). In the book of Acts, we see the Apostle Paul search the scriptures and open them for others. We hear that many believed because of this work (Acts 17:11-12). We read that "faith comes by hearing" (Rom 10:17), and we hear that all scripture is inspired by God (2 Tim 3:16). The scriptures illuminate the ways and will of God.

Thirdly, we wait in corporate worship and by partaking in the Lord's Supper. Worship is a key means by which God communes and communicates with us. The sacrament is an outward, visible means whereby God conveys God's nourishing, life-giving grace.

Some object by saying these means can overshadow our need to trust in God. Yes, we must trust in God. The means of grace lead us to this trust. By faithfully practicing these means, we come to desire God's blessings. God can and does use these means to open our hearts.

Others object that these means of grace promote "salvation by works." Do you know the meaning of this expression? In the writing of Paul, this phrase is used for those seeking to be saved by observing the ritual law of Moses or expecting salvation by proving their own righteousness. Attending to these means of grace is not the same as promoting "works." These means are ordained by God as ways for us to wait upon the Lord and cultivate expectant hearts.

A third objection is that Christ is the only means of grace. I answer that this is merely playing with words. Who denies this? Not me. Christ himself gave us means of grace. They are the means through which Christ calls us.

So, imagine a person going on their own way, not having God in their thoughts at all, and then God comes into their mind, perhaps by a sermon or conversation or perhaps by some awful event. Having a newfound desire to "flee from the wrath before them" and to "come into God's love," they inquire how this might be done. They find a preacher who speaks to the heart. They begin to search the scriptures. Perhaps they find some other books to help them as well. By all these means, the arrows of conviction sink deeper into the soul. They have a desire to meet with others in the congregation to pray and explore, even though they may be unsure of what to say at this point. They observe others going to the Lord's table and hear the words, "Do this." And they want to go forward.

This scenario is a real example of God's method to bring us into life. In varied ways, God uses all these means to lead and bless us. This is why we promote all the means God has ordained, remembering not to get stuck in the actions themselves and to see them as channels through which God generates renewal to our souls and brings us into true holiness.

If God's love flows into our hearts from these means, the means themselves will fade away to reveal the true glory. We will see, know, and feel that God is in all. We will then give God all the praise and let God be glorified in all things through Christ Jesus our Lord.

Amen.

"Maps, Means, and Methods"

Colossians 3:12-17

It was Thanksgiving afternoon, after we were all stuffed, when another ritual occurred at our house. Children and adults alike started going through all the Black Friday ads and making lists. My now-adult children still knew that their mother—not their father—would be up at four or so the next morning to meet with friends and would spend the whole day shopping. The moms and daughters who go on these yearly adventures will even spend time Thanksgiving night making a map. They are serious about this. And just so you know, my job is to hold down the fort, watch football, and eat leftovers while my wife, Dede, goes out and has all the fun.

Yes, this is that time of year when we make our lists and spend a lot of time thinking about what we want. I want us to compare and contrast that with thinking about what God

13

wants for us. The Greek word for prayer used most often in the scriptures means "advance desires." Prayer, at its core, is not telling God what we want as much as it is opening our lives to what God wants for us. God wants more for us. What might that be for you? The word "advent" means "to come." Advent is about God coming into our lives bearing divine gifts—gifts of hope, peace, joy, and love beyond compare. In our prayers and desires, are we focused on these gifts or on more mundane and finite desires?

Here's another example to compare and contrast. This time of year, many of us do a lot of searching. We go through ads and scroll through websites, searching for what we might want. Today, I want us to compare and contrast that searching with what John Wesley calls "searching the scriptures." We are invited to search for what we want in the scriptures and through our holy conversations around God's will. How much time are you devoting to that kind of searching?

This time of year, many of us will gain a few pounds. Christmas is a season of feasting and parties. At the church I serve, we gather for a movie night to watch *Elf* and feast upon the four main food groups according to the character Elf: candy, candy canes, candy corn, and syrup. Like Elf, we'll even try these four food groups on spaghetti. Doesn't that sound great? Yes, we will feast together many times throughout the holidays.

But now I want you to compare that scenario with receiving God's abundant, life-giving grace by receiving a small piece from a common loaf of bread. You don't get it all. You get to participate in something so much bigger than yourself. You get to be incorporated into God's family, called the body of Christ. At this table, abundance is expressed not by stuffing yourself but by taking on a small piece of what the Apostle Paul calls the "indescribable riches of God's grace." In this morsel is more abundance than we can comprehend.[8]

The sacrament of communion reminds us that God does not just say we are loved; God *shows* us. God "ADVENTures" into our world "in person" through our Savior, Jesus Christ, to give us this grace beyond measure. In the mystery of the gospel, this bread and cup become the body of Christ and the life of Christ for us. We physically take these blessings in, and they transform us spiritually.

So far, we've mentioned prayer, searching the scriptures, and Holy Communion. John Wesley called these the "means of grace." We can add others as well: holy conversation and conferencing, fasting, and works of mercy and service. These are the ordinary means, or ways, that God has given us to grow in the immeasurable riches of God's grace (Eph 2:7). We could also call these the "method of Methodism" or the map for our adventure. While God can work in extraordinary ways, most often, God works among us through ordinary channels to convey grace to us. God works through our gatherings, through water, bread, a cup, a word, and acts of love. God works through us.

In our scripture lesson from Colossians, the Apostle Paul calls us to practice these means of grace because they lead us into all that God wants for us. To use Paul's language, we are first called to "let the word of Christ dwell richly within us"—a beautiful phrase. Then, we "teach and admonish one another." We "sing hymns and spiritual songs with gratitude in our heart." In other words, we practice the methods God has given and follow the map Jesus has laid out. And when we do, what happens? Where does it all lead? The Apostle Paul gives a clear, direct answer. We grow in compassion, kindness, humility, and patience. We renew our commitment to bear one another in love and forgive one another. We put on the love that binds everything together in perfect harmony. That's what happens when we attend to the means of grace that God has given us.

I invite you to engage in some comparing and contrasting this season. You might, for example, focus on the lights and ornaments of the season, or you could let these lights and ornaments open you to the light of Christ. You might get so stressed about the meals that you miss the joy of gathering around the table. Compare those options. What do you really want, and what does God really want for you?

Compare and contrast. We can wish for things that bring temporary pleasure, things that break, fade, or go away, or we can put our hope in God, in the sure and certain hope rooted in what God has already done for us. We don't just wish for this; we anticipate it. We know these gifts of life and love will come, even into eternity. What do you really want? What map do you need to follow? What practices will lead you into all that God wants for you?

The last verse of our scripture lesson holds the key: "Whatever you do, in word or deed, do everything in the name of the Lord Jesus, giving thanks to God the Father through him." Amen.

Reflections for Personal Devotion and Discipling

1. What are the means of grace, and why do we call them "means?" What challenge does this concept raise for you?

   Often, Methodism is associated with the "means of grace" as outlined by John Wesley. These means include prayer, searching the scripture, holy conversation, communion, fasting, and works of justice and compassion. The early Methodists indeed attended to these in a disciplined and intentional way, and that's how the name "Methodist" came to be. It was originally a term of ridicule and derision, but over time, it became an honored term. We are able to grow in God's grace and become all that God has called us to be as we attend to these God-given means or methods in a disciplined and intentional way.

2. Why do we emphasize the "ordinary" ways in which God works? How does this illuminate the way you view your relationship with God?

   When it comes to spirituality, we often seek the extraordinary, and yet, God works most often through "ordinary channels to convey grace to us." God works through our weekly gatherings, through water, bread, a cup, a word, or an act of love. God works through us.

3. What is the connection between our outward means and methods and the method that God uses to save us and restore us to the image of God?

   Our outward means and methods are meant to illuminate the method of God used to restore us to the image of God. Amid the power of sin and death, God's method to save us is love, revealed supremely through Jesus Christ. God's method is to transform our hearts with this love and call us to spread this love into a world of need. If we try to hoard it or keep it to ourselves, this love will grow as stale as old bread. This love grows as it is shared. "We love because God first loved us" (1 John 4:19). The means of grace help us live out this calling.

17

4. How do the means of grace help us "wait on the Lord?" Why is waiting important?

Advent is a season of waiting, preparation, and anticipation. There is something deeply spiritual about this posture. We often hear people say, "We've been patient long enough," or "It's time to make a decision." In light of our need to fix things, the scriptures consistently call us to patience. For Wesley, patience is a "gracious temper," a fruit of the Spirit. It is the posture of holding the "middle way" between the extremes where we can stay connected to each other with humility and compassion.

5. The soul-searching question for us this season is this: What do you really want?

This time of year, we often make lists of what we want. It is a highly commercialized time that leads us to think about this question in materialistic terms. But what do we really want?

CHAPTER TWO

"The Scripture Way of Salvation"

(A devotional paraphrase)

Sermon 43 in The Sermons of John Wesley

"For by grace you have been saved through faith, and this is not your own doing; it is a gift of God."

Ephesians 2:8

Paraphrase of Wesley sermon

The intricacies and implications of religion can be so hard to understand. Questions lead to more questions. Diverse perspectives call for great discernment and even more love. It is as complicated as life itself. And yet, at its core, the true religion of Jesus Christ is so simple. It is exactly suited to connect to our narrow capacity for understanding spiritual truth and can be summed up in the words "salvation," "faith," and "grace." The purpose of God's work is salvation, and the way this comes is by grace through faith.

So, what is salvation? This sacred word first describes our deliverance from the powers of sin and death, and, secondly, it describes our being reconciled into God's life-giving love. To be sure, salvation is more than going to heaven. Throughout the scriptures, it is a present reality as well as a future reality. Salvation points to God's great work "from the first dawning of grace in the soul, till it is consummated in glory." Let's look at the "method" for how God brings this gift into the world and into our lives.

We must first understand that God is at work before we are ever aware of it. We call this dimension of God's work "preventing" or "prevenient grace." This is the grace that "goes before" us and prepares the way. God makes us aware of sin and the destruction it brings. God plants within us the seeds of mercy. God clears the way for the blessings of forgiveness and new life.

From this kindling work of God, we are led into the two dimensions of salvation directly proclaimed by the Apostles: justification and sanctification. "Justification" is another word for pardon or acquittal. It entails forgiveness of sins and implies our acceptance into God's family. It means to be made right, or aligned, with God. This justification is not achieved by anything we do. On our own, we fall way short. This justification comes as a gift purchased by the righteousness of Christ. To use the image of the court, Christ paid all penalties for our sins on the cross. To use the image of sacrifice, Christ gave his life so we might live. To use the image of victory, Christ opens the way of life for us. Justification describes what God has done FOR us.

The next dimension of salvation is called "sanctification." This word describes what God does IN us and THROUGH us. Sanctification is akin to the word "holy" and means to be set apart or devoted to God. We might make a list of all that is the opposite of holy: anger, greed, self-will, love of the world—all the dispositions that bring harm and division into the world. On the other side are all blessings that are sanctified, or holy: love, joy, peace, patience, kindness—all the dispositions that bring life into the world. As we are justified, or aligned, in relationship with God, we are moved to grow in this kind of holiness.

The moment we are "born from above," we experience both real transformation and relational transformation. The real transformation can be described as an inward renewal. We feel the love of God deep within. We know, beyond knowing, that God is with us, and nothing can separate us from God's love (Rom 8:31-34). We come to know Christ as our peace (Eph 2:14). This change is beyond argument, and no power in this world can take it away. Then comes relational change. The love we receive transforms the way we relate to others. We are moved "from an earthly, sensual, devilish mind into the mind that was in Christ Jesus" (Phil 2:5f).

As newly adopted children of God, we do not enter this reality fully mature. We start this transforming journey as "babes in Christ" (see 1 Cor 3:1f, Eph 4:15-16). Life gives us the opportunity to grow into the possibilities before us. From our perspective, this growth is not without pain. Even as we experience the grace of God, we still struggle with the passions that bring so much harm—self-will, anger, lust, and the like. But by grace, we know these will not conquer, even as they cause great turmoil.

To address this struggle, we are given means of grace. This is the next dimension of our "growth in salvation" (1 Pet 2:2). The means of grace, as they have been called for generations, can be divided into two categories. First is "works of piety," such as public prayer, family prayer, private prayer; receiving the Lord's Supper; searching the scriptures; and the discipline of fasting. Secondly, "works of mercy" include engaging in holy conversations, feeding the hungry, welcoming the stranger, and providing spiritual counsel. By the intentional and disciplined practices of these God-given means, we are able to grow "from grace unto grace" (John 1:16). We can "take up our cross" and deny ourselves of all that does not lead to God (Luke 9:23). We are given the strength to engage in good works. This is the "method" God has given us to grow in our salvation.

We do not practice this method to earn salvation or to merit blessings. To approach religion in that way is to turn God into our servant and the one who responds to us. This approach is the opposite of true faith, which is the next key concept to explore. The faith we proclaim does not begin with our trust, as some suppose, but with God's life-giving presence made known to us. First, God fills our hearts, and we come to know, in the deepest way, that we have been reconciled to God without our sins counting against us (2 Cor 5:18-19). God's love comes first (1 John 4:19). Knowing this love, we are able to respond with heartfelt trust and with a desire to share the same love we have received. As God's light fills our soul, we are able to move forward with deeply held assurance and confidence. This is life-giving faith. We may try not to believe at this point, but it proves impossible. God is a part of who we are and how we see reality.

Some argue that repentance, viewed as mere shame and sorrow, needs to precede faith. Repentance can manifest itself in this way, especially early in the journey, but at its core, this word means a "change of mind from above." It suggests a transformed perspective given from a source beyond us. Repentance is not a condition for salvation. Take the thief on the cross as an example. He was justified by faith, not by any work. The moment one believes, with or without fruit, that's when justification is given. We are blessed when life affords us the time to participate in this change and grow in the fruits of repentance.

As we follow this "way of salvation" through prevenient, justifying, and sanctifying grace, we can expect to be made perfect in this life. This often misunderstood term simply means to be made whole in love—for God, for self, and for neighbor. This blessing can come to us in an instant and often does. God's perfect love can be fulfilled in us; that is, it can be fully present and known. Every moment is ripe with the possibilities of us knowing about and sharing this love. Look for this gift every day. There will be moments when it will come. Look for this blessing just as you are, as a poor sinner with nothing to share but the grace of Christ. Let your inmost soul cry out, "Come in Lord Jesus with your everlasting love." This is our cry of praise on the way of salvation.

Amen.

Salvation Adventure

Ephesians 2:1-17

Believe this. Don't believe that. Do this. Don't *do* that. So often, when we talk about religion, we focus on what we do—our doctrines, our practices, and what we need to do to honor God. And it can become so complicated. We clutter our religious path to God with all kinds of rules, barriers, and codes to get through. At one level, this is the nature of religion in the world. We use religion in this way to divide the world between us and them. We make rules to keep others out—unless they are willing to look and act like us. We even use religion to start wars. But is this what we might call true religion?

John Wesley, the founder of the Methodist movement and the inspiration for this book, was bothered by this. True religion for him was (or is) not rooted in creeds or practices. It is rooted only in God's love for us. We are invited into a personal relationship with a living God who loves us before we ever do anything to deserve this love and who calls us to grow and share this same love with others. This is the religion revealed to us in Christ our Lord. It is a relationship more than it is a religion.

The word "advent" means "to come." Advent is a season in the church year where we "make the path straight," in the spirit of John the Baptist, for God to come into our lives. God comes to do one thing: to save. This is, in fact, what the name Jesus means. The word "save"—or "salvation"—can get so clouded with all the religious stuff we put on it. At the heart of this word is to be "whole" or "healed." The image of the original word "save" is the healing or mending of a wound. Although we don't use the word much anymore, in English, we still have the word "salve," which has the same meaning. A salve is an ointment used to heal a wound or a break in the skin. That's what it means to be saved.

To be saved is to know that our relationship with God is mended and healed. It is to know that we are not alone and that nothing in life or death can ever separate us from God's love. This life-giving relationship is not something we can create for ourselves. It is a gift given in pure and perfect love. In our lesson, the Apostle Paul uses the word "grace" to describe this gift. Grace is the gift that opens our hearts to wanting so much more than what we see before us.

The Apostle Paul then goes on to say that Jesus Christ is the embodiment of this gift to the world. Paul says that Christ is our peace. He not only brings peace. He *is* our peace. As Paul says, Jesus Christ comes to break down every dividing wall of hostility. Christ removes the barriers between us and God and between us as people. He saves us, reconciles us, heals us, and brings us together. As Paul says, in him we all have access to God.

As our peace, the Christ we worship is bigger than any of our human claims or doctrines, languages, styles of worship, or cultural expression. Christ can work through all of this. He can reveal true love through our finite attempts to worship. He can take all this and reconcile us to God and to each other in ways we can only begin to comprehend. Everything Christ does, or will do, is from pure and perfect love. We can trust that. This is what it means to say that

Christ is our peace—and we are bold enough to say—peace for the whole world.

We are invited to walk with Christ on this great adventure in salvation. John Wesley talked about this as the "scriptural way of salvation." Building upon the Apostle Paul's words, John Wesley described this way of God's grace with three key theological concepts: prevenient grace, justifying grace, and sanctifying grace.

The first feature of this "way" is God's prevenient grace. The word "prevenient" means to "go before." This first dimension of God's grace expresses how God is at work before we even know it. God is with us, calling us, making us aware, giving us directions, and opening our hearts to God's love before we do anything. God goes before and prepares the way.

Next is justifying grace, where God comes with mercy and forgiveness. By grace, we are justified, or aligned, in relationship with God. We might think of justified margins on a page or justice where all is made right. This justifying grace does not happen because of anything we do or don't do. It is a gift of pure and perfect love. Our response to this gift is faith and trust. We give our lives to the love we now know. That's faith. And then, when we find ourselves in this new relationship, we are led into sanctifying grace.

The word "sanctify" means to "be made whole." God works in us through the means of grace—through prayer, worship, holy conversations, and acts of mercy—to transform us from the inside out. As this grace is cultivated in us, the fruits of the Spirit grow—love, joy, peace, patience, kindness, goodness, gentleness, faithfulness, and temperance. These blessings become the fruit of our lives. They become the gifts along the way of salvation.

Are you ready to discover all that God wants for us? On this adventure, we will meet some major sources of inspiration. For example, we will join the shepherds who make their way to Bethlehem. In them, we see a dramatic transformation. These were rough and rugged men, men who had probably never had anything to do with babies. And yet, something happened to them. Their hearts were softened. They left their fields and flocks to "ooh and ahh" over a baby. Babies have a way of bringing out that kind of love. In gazing upon the Christ child, the shepherds not only saw him, but they also saw something new in themselves. They discovered the love of God.

You do not want to miss this adventure. The way is right before you. God has cleared the way. God's love is given first, and we are invited to respond. Then we are able to come to a personal, heartfelt trust in the God whose love is revealed in Christ Jesus our Lord. This love cannot be taken away by anyone or any force in this world. I invite you to take your next step, whatever that may be for you.

Amen.

Reflections for Personal Devotion and Discipling

1. Salvation is more than about going to heaven. It is a present and future reality. In what way are we being saved? What does salvation look like in this life?

   There are three key words to describe the way of God to us (or the adventure of God to us): prevenient grace, justifying grace, and sanctifying grace. Review what is said about these concepts. In another place, Wesley talked about this way of salvation by saying that prevenient grace is like the porch of a great mansion. Justifying grace is like the door. It is where we enter. Sanctifying grace is the opportunity to explore every room and every dimension and make it our home. That's a metaphor for this scriptural way of salvation.

2. Where does faith fit into this way of salvation? How does faith relate to love? How does faith lead us into love?

   We do not practice this method of faith to earn salvation. To approach religion in that way is to turn God into our servant and the one who responds to us. This is the opposite of true faith. Review the way faith is illuminated through a Wesleyan lens.

3. What does it mean to participate in sanctifying grace? Is it possible for us to practice holiness in this life, and what does that look like?

   There are Protestant theologies that focus on being a "forgiven sinner" but do not go much further. If justification is described as a doorway, for many, this door leads into the church where obedience, outward morality, and perhaps even judgment of others are seen as proof of salvation. In this theology, the call is to practice outward obedience until we make it to heaven, where we will be transformed. As Wesleyans, we are more optimistic, for the door of justification leads us into the kin-dom of God, where we can grow and become all that God created us to be. Our hearts are transformed along the way. As we follow this way of salvation through prevenient, justifying, and sanctifying grace, we can expect God's love to be perfected within us. We trust that we are being transformed, from one degree to another, into the image of Christ. As Wesleyans, we are optimistic about what is possible as we intentionally engage in the means of grace that God has given us.

4. Read the example of the shepherds. What does their transformation say for us today? How do we need to be transformed?

Repentance is a needed ingredient if we are to experience the blessings of salvation. At its core, it is a "change of mind from above." It suggests a transformed perspective. Ponder the transformation within the shepherds who made their way to Bethlehem. How were they able to see things differently?

CHAPTER THREE

"Circumcision of the Heart"

(A devotional paraphrase)

Sermon 17 in The Standard Sermons of John Wesley

"True circumcision is a matter of the heart—it is spiritual and not literal. Such a person receives praise not from others but from God."

Romans 2:29

Paraphrase of Wesley sermon

Preaching Christianity's most basic and essential practices can sound strange to many—perhaps even foolish. Keeping Christianity at a distance, it can be nice to hear stories of Jesus and his resurrection, but when we move to the consequences of this faith for our own lives, it can become disturbing rather quickly. To suggest, for example, that we are called to die to this world and live wholly to God is hard on our natural ears if we are not awakened to the spiritual senses given by God.

The distinguishing mark of a true follower of Christ is what the Apostle Paul calls the "circumcision of the heart." This metaphor reminds us that life-giving faith is not found in outward circumcision, baptism, or any other outward ritual or act; rather, it is found within. To put it another way, the distinguishing mark of Christian faith is a change of heart; it is the deep inward awareness beyond logic or outward senses that our spirit is being renewed in the image of the One who created it. From this change of heart, the fruits of holiness grow and bring blessings to the world. Yes, this may sound foolish to those who have yet to experience this life-giving grace.

At the root is a change from arrogance and self-will to a sense of humility and humble gratitude. We let go of all arrogant claims to our own wisdom. We recognize that we are "poor in spirit," lacking the resources needed to save ourselves. We accept that we are human and not God (note the similarities between the words "human" and "humility). Our spiritual senses are opened to the truth that, without God working in our lives and transforming us from the inside out, we can do nothing but add sin to sin.

Another word for this dimension of the fruits of holiness is "faith." Faith is so much more than affirming a doctrinal position. Faith opens our hearts to God's transforming work. It overturns "the prejudices of our corrupt reason." It reverses "the maxims revered by those who focus on their own power." This faith leads us beyond our senses, beyond our inward passions, to a light that empowers us to walk not by sight but with the Spirit there to direct our steps and govern our desires. In faith, we know that God, in Christ, has reconciled *me*—even *me*—and has entrusted to *me* the ministry of reconciliation. Knowing this in the heart changes everything.

Those who are born of God through this gift of faith also have "hope." This is the next gift implied in the circumcision or change of the heart. This hope is more than a wish or dream. It is a certain confidence that we are now on a path that leads to life. By this anchor, we are able to keep steady amid "the waves of this troublesome world." We know that strength comes for the race set before us and victory will be given.

Confirmed and strengthened, we not only renounce the works of darkness ("out-there" or in others) but turn inward to face our own appetites and affections that draw us away from God. As the Apostle John says, "Who has this hope, purifies themselves as he is pure" (1 John 3:3). In our daily disciplines, we work to purge our souls from every passion that defiles them, from every lust, envy, and malice driven by flesh without spirit. This is our Christian warfare. We engage in this work daily, trusting in our hearts that our labor is not in vain. This is our sure and certain hope.

To this point, we may have deep humility, steadfast faith, and much hope but still lack the "most excellent gift," the end, or purpose, of all commandments: love. Love is the essence of all that is good and just and holy (Phil 4:8). Without love, we have nothing (1 Cor 13:1-3).

As we often say, love is "The royal law of heaven and earth." It comes to us from God on its way to others. The Creator's love leads us to love the creature and creation, and as we do this, we are led back to the Creator. In this movement, love grows around us and in our hearts.

Humility, faith, hope, and love. The Holy Spirit is at work empowering the transformation of our souls. We get to participate in this work but be warned. It is not easy. We cannot hope for these blessings to be fully present (or fulfilled) without pain. No child of Adam and Eve can expect to see and know the kingdom of God without striving, without agonizing first to "enter by the narrow gate" and to "take up the cross daily." Without this struggle amid this finite and frail life, we cannot even dream of shaking off our "old opinions, passions, and tempers." Without the work of the Holy Spirit and our consent, we would never even see this need.

And yet, through this struggle comes true joy. We are able to know that nothing can separate us from God's love, not even death itself (Rom 8:31-34). We are able to know that God is with us and, as "Emmanuel," will see us through. We have an inheritance that is incorruptible and undefiled (1 Pet 1:4). In this, we can rejoice in all circumstances, knowing the victory has already been won (Phil 4:4).

Don't let certain theological deceivers convince you that this struggle is too much and leads only to works righteousness or that we must wait to be made perfect. God is at work now, giving us this joy now, even as we struggle in this life. This work in the heart is at the heart of true religion. True religion is not in the resources and rituals, as helpful as these can be. True religion is about what God is doing in our lives. It is about God's transforming grace that comes into the world by way of the heart through Jesus Christ our Lord.

Are you being transformed, as Paul says, from one degree of glory to another (2 Cor 3:18), from fear to faith, from greed to generosity, from anger to mercy, from death to life? Is that happening in you? It is ironic; to build religion on rituals and outward appearance is to build on the proverbial sand, as Jesus says. When the storms come, outward faith crumbles. To turn to the heart and open yourself daily to God's transforming grace is to build your life on solid rock (Matt 7:24-26). Then the rains come, winds blow, and storms threaten, but the temple stands. This, says Wesley, is the "short and plain account of true religion." God wants to connect with you in your heart. No one can do this for you or tell you exactly what it will mean for you. God wants this kind of relationship with you. God is big enough to do this with each of us. That's true religion.

Amen.

"Change of Heart"

Matthew 1:18-24

They are among the most well-known Christmas characters. We have Mary and Joseph, Frosty and Rudolph, and characters like George and Clarence. In case you haven't seen *It's a Wonderful Life*, here is a spoiler alert. George learns many important lessons. His narrow, materialistic perspective on life has led him to believe he has failed and is worthless. And just as George resolves to give up, the angel Clarence enters his life, and he begins to see it all from a whole new perspective. I wonder if, or when, that has happened to you.

John Wesley, the founder of a revival movement in 18th-century England and whose sermons are a part of our doctrine, was concerned about the question, "What is religion all about?" How might we define "true religion?" Wesley was concerned about how easy it is for us to get hung up on the rituals, creeds, and institutions and miss what is truly meant to be at the heart of it all—love, peace, joy, and gifts that come to us as we live in a relationship with a living God who is involved in our lives. True religion is not about "religion" in terms of institutions and practices; it is about relationship, a relationship with a living God. True religion is God's love in the heart radiating out to the world. Doctrines, practices, and institutions are important resources but are not at the heart of religion. When we make these things our focus, we start to bring the opposite of love, peace, and joy into the world. Religion becomes a disease.

True religion is about love, not as an abstract concept but as love that transforms us from the inside out. This love transforms us from arrogance to humility, where we accept that we are human and not God. We are transformed from judgment to compassion, from greed to grace, from fear to faith. We want to give our lives to the love we have received. We have the strength to do more than renounce the darkness "out-there," and we can also honestly face what is going on within us and purge our souls of all that leads to darkness and death—lust, envy, self-centeredness, fear, malice of all kinds. We find ourselves wanting to engage in the means of grace—prayer, worship, reading scripture, holy conversation, acts of mercy. When God gets into our lives, we discover joy amid our struggles.

In our scripture for this chapter, we encounter Joseph, who has found himself in a big mess. We are told from the beginning that Joseph was a righteous man, so he wanted to do the right thing amid this mess. According to the legal and social conventions of their day, Joseph, Mary, and their families were in a legal agreement moving towards marriage. And because of this agreement, Joseph had to choose between a public or private divorce. A public split would have shamed Mary and enabled him to keep his reputation in place. He would have been able to say, "She did this to me, and I am the righteous one." A private divorce would bring scandal on him because people would wonder why he didn't live up to the agreement. This was his "rock and a hard place" choice.

We all know "righteous" people who would advocate the public route. After all, given the circumstances, Mary deserved to be humiliated. Joseph, however, had a different sense of righteousness. His understanding of what is right was rooted less in the law and more in what it means to be "gracious and merciful, slow to anger, and abounding in steadfast love." In the Hebrew scriptures, we hear this description over and over again. In this struggle, Joseph asked himself how he could fulfill that kind of righteousness in the midst of his deep pain.

Note the way it is worded in the scripture. We read, "Just when he resolved to do this," something happened. Joseph had an encounter with an angel of the Lord, and his heart and life were changed. He began to see this whole situation from a new perspective, even beyond his graceful understanding of righteousness. Joseph came to know Emmanuel as a name and a reality. The name Emmanuel means "God with us." Joseph came to know that God was with him—actively with him and at work in his life. That changed everything for him.

In the spirit of Emmanuel, of a living God being with us and at work in our everyday lives, I invite you to focus this week on the everyday ways in which this change of heart can happen for anyone listening and whose hearts are open to more than the mundane before us.

Perhaps you have believed at some point that your life had no purpose and you were worthless. And just when you resolved to give up, something happened that helped you see life from a new perspective and that you could start fresh with a new calling—not unlike George from *It's a Wonderful Life*.

Or perhaps you became obsessed with a person you

believe had wronged you in some way, and just as you resolved to get even, something happened that moved you to a posture of forgiveness.

Or perhaps you looked at your finances and took to heart the commercials that can tap into your desires for acceptance and worth, and just as you resolved to make a purchase that would get your life out of balance between what you do for yourself and what you do for the glory of God, something happened that awakened in you a desire to live with more balance and to be more generous.

Or perhaps you wanted to talk to someone about something important, but you were scared about how they might react. Just as you resolved to bury it inside, something happened that gave you the courage to start the conversation.

Have you experienced this? Are you being transformed, as Paul says, "from one degree of glory to another," from fear to faith, from greed to generosity, from anger to mercy, from death to life? Is that happening in you? Wesley calls this transformation of heart "the short and plain account of true religion." At the heart of it all is a relationship with a living God who is there for you. The right, or righteous, thing to do is to listen and let Emmanuel walk with you on this adventure that brings true joy, even amid the mess.

Amen.

Reflections for Personal Devotion and Discipling

1. What does it mean to say that true religion is a matter of the heart and not outward practices?

For Wesley, true religion is a change of heart. It is a heart right with God and with our fellow human beings. To illuminate this point, Wesley relies on the Apostle Paul's image of the "circumcision of the heart." The key word is "heart." Life-giving faith is not found in outward circumcision, baptism, or any other outward ritual or act; rather, it is found within. To build religion on rituals and outward appearance is to build on the proverbial sand, as Jesus says. When the storms come, outward faith crumbles. To turn to the heart and open yourself daily to God's transforming grace is to build your life on solid rock (Matt 7:24-26).

2. How do we know this change is from God? What are the outcomes of this change?

God brings a transformation from arrogance and self-will to humility and gratitude to make one of many comparisons. Humility is perhaps the first sign of a heart transformed by God. Next, God opens our hearts to faith, a faith beyond senses and sight. We know God deep within and give our lives to God's love. Next, our hearts are opened to a hope that is beyond wishes and dreams. We are given the confidence to know that nothing can separate us from God's love. And love is the "royal law," the key outcome of a transformed heart. Without this love, we are nothing. Important byproducts of this love are joy and peace. This, says Wesley, is the "short and plain account of true religion."

3. How does this transformation happen? Where and/or how have you experienced it? How might we keep the vision of transformation before us?

The Apostle Paul says we are being transformed from one degree of glory to another (2 Cor 3:18), from fear to faith, from greed to generosity, from anger to mercy, from death to life. Is that happening in you? As Methodists, we are optimistic about this possibility. Review how this transformation happens within the teachings.

4. Read the story of Joseph. What does his change of heart reveal to us about God and our calling?

Joseph was a righteous man, but we are told that in his encounter with the angel, his whole understanding of righteousness changed. What was this change? What are the implications of this for us?

CHAPTER FOUR

"On Charity"
(A devotional paraphrase)

From Sermon 91 in The Sermons of John Wesley

If I speak in the tongues of mortals and of angels, but do not have love, I am a noisy gong or a clanging cymbal. And if I have prophetic powers, and understand all mysteries and all knowledge, and if I have all faith, so as to remove mountains, but do not have love, I am nothing.

1 Corinthians 13:1-3

Paraphrase of Wesley sermon

We know that all scripture is inspired by God. Yet, some passages take hold of our conscience in a special way and serve as master texts to help us interpret all revelatory claims, even those in scripture. Next to what Jesus calls the summary of it all—Love God and love your neighbor as a part of yourself—our text for today would be at the top of this list. I have heard people of other faith traditions even say that this is as good a description of true religion as anything they have seen. I once heard Dr. Nunes, a Spanish-Jewish physician living in Savannah, Georgia, say he wished these words could be written in gold and that every Jew would carry them wherever they went. He claimed that these words contain the whole of true religion. I agree.

St. Paul's word "agape" is often translated as "love." This

is true of the Tyndale Bible, the first English translation, and those later authorized by King Henry, Queen Elizabeth, and King James I. In 1649, printers of the parliament made a subtle change, using the Latin word "charity" instead of the English word "love." In my opinion, this was an unfortunate change. Based on the common understanding of "charity," many have been misled to believe that this word refers only to outward actions, acts of kindness, and handouts without relationship. If the proper word "love" had been retained, there would be no room for this misrepresentation.

What kind of love is represented here? I am convinced that Saint Paul is speaking directly about our love of neighbor, acknowledging that this love can only spring from the love of God. It flows from the faith that knows, deep in the heart, that God was in Christ reconciling the world to Godself. It is this love that we want for all other souls. We might say it like this: "God's love comes to us, always on its way to someone else."

What are the properties of this love, the fruits of this love? This is a continuous theme in Wesley's sermons, so before we focus on the first three verses, here is a summary.

First, "Love is not puffed up," to use the old language. It is humble, patient, and kind. It does not insist on its own way. It is not arrogant or rude. It is willing to be a servant of all. It magnifies God, not self or our own opinions.

Secondly, "Love is not easily provoked," to use the King James language. The word "easily" has been added to the text, presumably because Paul did seem to be provoked at times. See, for example, his disagreement with Barnabas in Acts 15. Yet, this qualification with the word "easily" is unnecessary.

We may be provoked, but love is not provoked, even if we give into temperaments contrary to God's will. For a more generous read, we could take the view that Paul did not speak to Barnabas or others in a way contrary to the law of love and remains a strong example to us of "humble boldness."

Thirdly, love is "long-suffering," to use the old word again. It suffers "with" or has compassion for all. The word "compassion" literally means "with suffering." We are called to compassion for all the pain of the world, always seeking to work for good. Thus, in love, we do not insist on our own way or work to have our opinions affirmed, not before we fully learn how to love amid our differences. These verses show the heart of holiness and our witness to the world.

We now turn to the first verses of this poem in 1 Corinthians 13. These beautiful words contain a sharp edge of warning that we must not overlook. We may speak with great power concerning the nature, attributes, and works of God, but without humble, gentle, patient love, we are no better, in the judgment of God, than a clanging cymbal. We may have the gift of prophecy and understand all mysteries, but without humility and gentleness, we gain nothing. We may have great faith, even to remove mountains, but if our faith does not work for love and does not produce holiness, it profits nothing. All faith that does not reveal love—to "friend or foe, Christian, Jew, heretic, or pagan"—is not the faith of Christ.

To illustrate this warning of love, I recall a remarkable tract from Dr. Geddes, a civilian who was an envoy from Queen Anne to the Court of Portugal. He was present during an "Act of Faith" when Roman Inquisitors burned heretics alive. One of the persons executed had been confined to the dungeons and had not seen the sun for many years. When he was brought to the bench, he cried out, "O how can anyone who sees that glorious luminary worship any but the God that made it!" His body was then prepared to be burned. What did this poor man feel at that moment? If he said in his heart, "Father, forgive them, for they know not what they do," he undoubtedly was delivered into paradise. If, on the other hand, he cherished resentment in his heart, we cannot say with confidence that he was ready for paradise—not without the transformation that can only come from the grace of God. These beautiful words ring with a warning. Even if "I hand over my body to be burned" but am still under the power of pride, anger, or fretfulness, "it profits me nothing." Even this kind of martyrdom will not overcome the need for our hearts to be transformed and saved. That's why Jesus came—and continues to come—into our lives.

From these powerful words, we must conclude that true religion is nothing less than holy temperaments, described here with the word "love." Consequently, all other religions, whatever we call it—Paganism, Islam, Judaism, Christianity—"whether Popish or Protestant, Lutheran or Reformed," without these temperaments as described here— without love—they are "lighter than vanity itself."

Hear this, all who are called Methodists! You speak of salvation by faith. You maintain that we are justified by faith without the works of the law. And you are right to do so. But this faith is still the handmaid to love. Our faith— or trust in the love God has given—is meant to soften our hearts and save us first from all unholy temperaments such as pride, passion, impatience, and all arrogance of spirit.

Guard against the strong delusion that we can indulge these temperaments and still dream we are on the way to heaven. Let everyone with a soul to be saved see that you are secure in this one point. Beyond all the words, knowledge, works, and even faith, let us all hold fast to the "one thing needful": humble, gentle, patient love. By the grace of Christ and through the work of the Holy Spirit, this is what is needed to receive our place in the kingdom that has been prepared for us from the foundation of the world.

Amen.

"The Reason for the Season"

John 1:1-14

I bet you have heard the saying, "Jesus is the reason for the season." From our perspective, this is true. From our perspective, Jesus can get lost amid our traditions and gatherings, gift-giving and getting. Remembering Jesus may be the best thing we can do for ourselves. In this sense, it is good to remember that Jesus is the reason for the season. But that is from our human perspective. I wonder, though, what God's perspective on Christmas is.

From God's perspective, WE are the reason for the season. God looked upon our condition and saw darkness in need of light, death in need of life, deep loneliness, and longing in need of love. And so, WE are the reason for Christmas. Christmas is all about God coming to us.

The Gospel of John starts its version of the Christmas story by saying, "In the beginning was the Word, and the Word was with God." The Word! In the original language, this word is "Logos," which means to take chaos and order it into something meaningful. The English word "logic" comes from this word. It is translated as "word" because that's how God creates and gives life and takes chaos and gives it meaning. God creates by speaking it all into existence, according to the first "word" in the Bible. Genesis 1:1 says, "In the beginning, God created the heavens and the earth." John makes the connection by saying, "In the beginning," God's word—God's creating, life-giving power—was there, and all things came into being through God.

Now, that kind of fancy theological talk is all well and good, but it still leaves God "out-there" in the realm of theory and ideas, not in the realm of relationship. And so, God gives Christmas to us. John proclaims that the "Word became flesh and dwelt among us, full of grace and full of truth." It is a reference to Jesus, who, from our perspective, is the reason for the season, but from God's perspective, is the one sent to us because we need to know that God is with us and will see us through. From God's perspective, WE are the reason for Christmas.

So, let us further explore the deep implications of this gift from God. By our logos, or logic, we like to divide and compartmentalize. This means we even like to keep God "up-there," so to speak, and out of our daily business. It's just easier and more comfortable that way. We come to church for a dose of spirituality. Then we go "out-there" and live our lives. We see a thread of connection, but by our logic, we can too easily keep these dimensions in separate compartments. By this human logic, we separate sacred and secular, spiritual and worldly, soul and body.

And here's where this logic can get us in trouble. When we feel the need to be more spiritual, we often think we must be less human and less worldly. We might think, "If only I could get away from all the worldly stuff, then I might be able to see God." That way of thinking, that form of logic, is so ingrained in our culture. But then Christmas comes. God's logos, God's logic, breaks in. For Christmas people, spirituality is recognizing that God enters into our lives— into the mess of it all, into the joys of it all, into the pain of it all. God wants to share gifts of light, love, and life right there amidst it all. That's where we need to look for these blessings: right in the very midst of our daily lives.

The big theological word to describe this involvement in our lives is "incarnation." This word describes something spiritual taking on physical form and becoming incarnate, visible, and real in the world. Love, for example, is just a theoretical, abstract, spiritual concept that becomes real or "incarnate" through acts of kindness, patience, and compassion to build upon the Apostle Paul's description of love. Love becomes life-giving when it takes physical form with a humility that does not "insist on its own way." Love comes to life in those interested in building relationships and being *with* others, not *over* others. These are the virtues that make love incarnate in the world.

In John Wesley's sermon "On Charity," which we are using to inspire us in this chapter, Wesley explores the words from Paul in 1 Corinthians, Chapter 13 (Wesley draws upon these words repeatedly). In this sermon, Wesley points out that the first English translation of the scriptures translated the Greek word "agape" as "love." Then, somewhere along the way—and there are no clear records when, who, or how this happened—the word "charity" began to be used instead of "love." This became the word in the authorized King James translation, and Wesley was one of the first to call for a revival of the word "love." He argued that the word "charity" allows us to think of love as a "handout." It allows us to keep our distance. We can do something nice but don't have to get involved. God wants more for us—and gives more to us—than charity. "Love" is the better word. In this great passage, it is made clear that without love, we have nothing.

We can have all faith, knowledge, and great power, but without love, we have nothing. It is beautiful and poetic but also a warning to us. Focusing on anything less than God's love is done at the peril of our well-being.

Christmas is all about the incarnation of God's love. It is all about God dwelling among us and with us to bring love to the world. And it all starts in our hearts. God wants to make a home right in our hearts and fill this home with the light of love, a light so powerful that no form of darkness or death can overcome it, as the Gospel of John says. This is the blessing of Christmas.

At Christmas, we love to shine the spotlight on Jesus and say, "Jesus is the reason for the season." Today, let us know that God shines the light of heaven on us and says, "Oh, how I love you. You are the reason for it all."

Amen.

Reflections for Personal Devotion and Discipling

1. How do we interpret scripture? What is the primary purpose of scripture?

A popular method for interpreting scripture has been called "proof-texting" or "selective literalism." By this method, we can prove almost anything and confirm most biases. As Wesleyans, we promote a different hermeneutic, or method, for interpreting. Wesley calls us to filter all scriptures through key passages that take hold of our conscience in a special way and help us interpret all revelatory claims, even those in scripture. Jesus himself used this method when he summarized all the law and the prophets with the call to love God and our neighbor as a part of ourselves. Jesus interpreted scripture through this lens. For Wesley, another interpretive key would be found in the definition of love from 1 Corinthians 13. Wesley calls this love the "chief of all graces" and the "royal law." We are called to assess all scripture through these interpretive keys. Key passages include Matthew 22:37-40 (and parallels), 1 Corinthians 13:1-8, and 1 John 4:7-12, 19.

It is a sign of inspiration that our predecessors did not "clean up" the scriptures. We have passages that are problematic and express culturally conditioned values. We have passages that do not fit with the will of God as we have come to know it through the lens of Christ. With the wisdom of passages that express the timeless values of God as discerned through the ages, we are able to engage all of scripture and struggle together to discern how we might live faithfully and fruitfully in the context we are given. As Wesleyans, we honor the whole, notice the context, explore the history, understand the words, and seek God's intended message, not necessarily in the words but through them.[9]

2. What is the best definition of the Greek word "agape": love or charity? What is the difference?

Wesley argues against the authorized translation, arguing for "love" over "charity." He sees charity as something akin to handouts. Love demands a relationship where we can practice patience, kindness, and a humility that does not insist on its own way. In a world bent on division and judgment, the practice of this kind of love is so relevant and needed.

3. What are the challenges of love? What does it mean to say that faith works for love?

In this sermon, Wesley quickly moves to the first few verses of this biblical passage where Paul firmly warns us that we have nothing without love. All faith, belief, and even sacrifice are in service to love.

4. How is this love offensive to those invested in the ways of the world? What are the implications of this love in how we view religion and politics?

This talk of love may sound sweet and nice, but it reveals an edge. Love can be offensive, especially for those with the power and privileges to protect. This love turns the world upside down.

5. What does it mean to say that Jesus is God incarnate? How are we to love incarnately and contextually?

Reread the section on how Christmas is about the incarnation of God's love. So often, we leave God "out-there" in the realm of theory and ideas. In Christ, the "Word became flesh and dwelt among us, full of grace and truth." What does this mean for how we are to live our lives?

CHAPTER FIVE

"On Zeal"
(A devotional paraphrase)

Sermon 92 in The Sermons of John Wesley

"It is fine to be zealous, provided the purpose is good."

Galatians 4:18

Paraphrase of Wesley sermon

Zeal. Enthusiasm. Passion. Motivation. Determination. Whatever word we use, this dynamic is so important to our well-being. Without zeal, it is impossible to progress in our faith or service to others. And yet, nothing has done more disservice to religion or caused more mischief to humankind. Gone astray, zeal can become fanaticism or extremism. It can manifest itself as self-righteousness, judgment, revenge, and even war. Terrible instances have occurred throughout history. It was zeal that kindled fires in our nation during the reign of bloody Queen Mary. It was zeal that turned provinces in France into fields of blood. It was zeal that led to the horrid massacre in Ireland. Zealousness has been a part of our history going back to the persecution of the early church.

The original word for "zeal" suggests "heat." When figuratively applied, it suggests a boiling of emotions or desires. It can easily take the form of prejudice or anger. So, our question becomes, how do we distinguish true Christian zeal from its various counterfeits? It is not easy to do. The deceitfulness of the human heart makes it so easy for us to justify our passions. This sermon clearly establishes that zeal must be rooted in love. Without love, zeal is a harmful and destructive display (see 1 Cor 13:1-3). Misplaced zeal leads to the opposite of true holiness.

Love is the key. To understand this concept, the best place to start is in the thirteenth chapter of First Corinthians. Here we learn that true love is patient and kind. It is not "puffed up" and does not insist on its own way. Like wax melting at the fire, the sacred flame of God's love melts all turbulent passions, all anger and arrogance, and leaves our souls in peace—peace with God and goodwill for all, even in our human differences. We are called to be zealous for this peace.

Healthy zeal within the church has several components that must be connected properly. As a visual exercise, let us draw these components in concentric circles to show how this works. The first circle represents how God's love for us is at the center, the core. In this love, God gave his son that we might have eternal life. In this love, we are able to know God and know that nothing in life or death can separate us from God's love. This love is at the heart of it all.

In the second circle encompassing this core are all *holy temperaments*—patience, gentleness, kindness, faithfulness, temperance, and all virtues within the "mind of Christ." These characteristics describe how God's love manifests through us.

In the next concentric circle are *works of mercy*, where we exercise all holy temperaments and give outward witness to

the love of God. In the next outer circle, we find *works of piety*—
reading the scriptures; public, family, and private prayer;
receiving the Lord's Supper; fasting; and abstinence. The last
concentric circle represents the church—the one body gathered
together with our diversity of gifts, perspectives, opinions, and
callings. We might add lines radiating outward like the sun
to this set of circles. We are always called to move outward in
love. God's love always comes to us on its way to others.

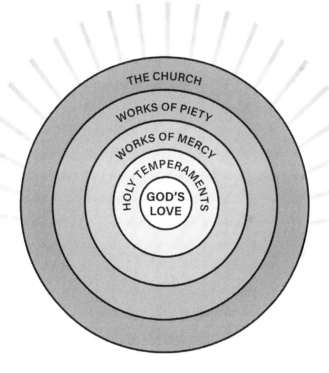

This image shows the various dimensions of true
religion in their proper order. We see that zeal is good
only insofar as it flows from God's love. If it flows from
any other dimensions, it only brings harm into the world.
For example, if we focus on how to pray or how to take

communion and use our zeal to promote our opinions and to divide or exclude, then our zeal only brings disease into the body. In this comparative analysis, even prayer and reading scripture must be postponed when we are called to help our neighbor because *works of mercy* are closer to the center than *works of piety*. And we can't stop there. As zealous as we might be for works of mercy, we should be more zealous for the holy temperaments needed for planting and promoting God's goodwill in the world: patience, kindness, humility. These fruits should be at the forefront of our minds when we lie down and rise up, when we work and play.

Our highest zeal is reserved for love, the "chief of all graces," the "highest perfection in heaven and earth." All outward works, all holy temperaments are to serve this love at the heart of it all. Let us all "press on to this prize of our high calling from God in Christ Jesus our Lord" (Phil 3:13-15; see also Col 3:12-17).

Here are some implications of this holistic perspective. We first note that hatred of every kind is the opposite of Christian zeal. If zeal is connected to love, then all bitterness, jealousy, bigotry, and persecution are absolutely inconsistent with it. Let none of these unholy temperaments be disguised to infiltrate the holy community and bring their disease and destruction.

Likewise, we cannot confuse zeal with anger, judgment, or personal passion. Too often, zeal is assessed by how much these temperaments are expressed. This assessment is a delusion. Passion is as inconsistent with true zeal as light is with darkness or heaven is with hell. Someone might say, "But I feel strongly about this," or "This is my passion." If it gets in the way of love, then it is sin. If you do not repent, it will "sink you lower than the grave," where there is much zeal of this sort.

Next, we cannot confuse zeal with discontent and impatience. How often do we hear so-called "Godly" people telling us that they are out of patience and so upset by the actions of others? Fretting at sin is a type of sin and has no connection with the true zeal of the gospel.

It follows that enthusiasm for theological opinions is not Christian zeal. How many thousands of lives have been cast away by those who were zealous for the ways of Rome or against the different opinions of other Christians? This zeal has no place in heaven, for only love is there.

Without zeal, we cannot advance in faith or fruits. But be aware of its power. God has given us the means to channel our zeal into true faithfulness and fruitfulness. Practice these means. If we don't, the result can be devastating. Above all, be zealous for the love that illuminates God. God is love, and those who dwell in love dwell in God and God in them (1 John 4:8). Count all things as loss compared to this. Even if you give all you have to feed the poor and even deliver your body to be martyred but do not have humble, gentle, patient love, you have nothing. Let this truth be deeply engraved on your heart!

Amen.

Christmas Eve:
"The Great Christmas Blessing"

1 Corinthians 13:1-8 and Luke 2:1-14

Each week, our youth groups gather in a circle with arms crossed and linked and give each other this blessing: "The Lord bless you and keep you. The Lord make his face to shine upon you and be gracious unto you. The Lord lift up his countenance upon you and give you peace." This blessing is straight from the scripture, found in the book of Numbers, Chapter 6.

Now, let us think about what it means to be blessed today. In our culture, blessings tend to be tied to whether we are naughty or nice. In other words, blessings come to those who are good and somehow deserving. Depending on what we do, we are either blessed or cursed; we are on the naughty or nice list. That's a popular way to understand this concept of blessing, but it is not completely biblical.

Here's the "big idea" I want us to understand on this Christmas Eve. The Hebrew word for "blessed" or "blessing" comes from the root word meaning "to kneel" or "to bow down." We might think of people kneeling before a king. To bless in this sense means to show honor and respect. To bless is to bow down before another and say, "I want to be a part of your life. I want what is good for you. I submit my life to you and want to share in your hopes and desires for the world." That's what it means to bless another in this biblical sense.

So, here is the most interesting thing about this

concept—and I hope this blows your mind or shakes up your spirit. Over and over again in the Bible, we see that God is the one doing the blessing. God is the one "kneeling" before us, "bowing down" to us, "submitting" to us, and "wanting what is good" for us. Think about this. The God of all creation, of billions of galaxies, where every grain of sand is known, is also big enough to bow down before you and say, "I honor you; I want to be a part of your life."

This truth comes to life in its most supreme form in the manger of Bethlehem. The birth of Jesus represents God on bended knee, coming down to us, kneeling before us, and saying, "I love you." In Jesus, God comes into our lives and says, "I want to be a part of your life." From the manger to the cross and through the cross, we see God bending down to us, coming all the way into our joys and sorrows, our triumphs and struggles, our life and death, showing us over and over again that nothing in life or death can separate us from God's love.

The shepherds learned quickly. These men probably had never had much to do with babies. And yet they were told to go to Bethlehem and bow before a baby. This was so counter to who they were, and yet they obeyed. They bowed down before this baby, and in the reflection of this infant, they could see something new in themselves. They discovered something about love. That can also happen to us when we bow down before a baby. We learn a lot about what is at the core of it all: love.

The Apostle Paul teaches us the virtues of this love. Paul reminds us that "love is patient." Babies teach us a lot about patience. "Love is kind," says the Apostle. We can't help but learn something about kindness and gentleness when we hold a baby. Paul goes on to say, "Love is not arrogant or rude; it does not insist on its own way. Imagine insisting on your own way with a baby; it does not work. Babies teach us a lot about love and how we are to interact with one another as children of God. I suspect this is why God chose to reveal his love in this way.

Committing to our religious views makes it easy for us to become zealous for the wrong things. John Wesley talked a lot about this in the sermon we are using to inspire us in this chapter. It is easy for us to get our priorities out of order and focus on *how* we worship rather than *who* we worship or to focus on our opinions about what is right rather than coming together for holy conversation where we can learn the right way to treat one another. As Paul says in this beautiful poem in 1 Corinthians 3, without love, we have nothing. Even if we have the faith to move mountains, it means nothing if not done in and for love. The hope of God is that this word will bless you and transform our hearts.

This Christmas Eve, some of you will have the opportunity to hold a baby or a child and bow to them. Others of you might call a child or loved one, hold the hand of someone you love for a moment, or make eye contact across the room. Whenever this moment comes for you, I invite you to whisper, "The Lord bless you."

I invite all of you to hear and feel deep in your heart the heavenly chorus proclaim this blessing to you as well: "The Lord bless you and keep you. The Lord make his face to shine upon you and be gracious unto you. The Lord lift up his countenance (his strength) upon you, and give you peace," "For unto you, is born this day, a Savior who is Christ the Lord."

Amen.

Reflections for Personal Devotion and Discipling

1. Reread the key passages on love listed here. What stands out for you? What challenges you? How do these passages connect to Christmas for you? What do they illuminate about Christmas?

We have heard that Methodism, or Wesleyan theology, can be summed up by the word "grace." As a theological concept to describe how God responds to our sin, this is a good word. However, from the standpoint of action and practicing faith, the word "love" is used as much as ten times more than "grace" in Wesley's writings. Love is the royal law of heaven and earth, the one thing that endures forever, the sum of all the law and the prophets. Love is at the very heart of it all. In other places, Wesley calls us to interpret all scripture through the lens of God's love.

2. What is the relationship between love and holiness? What do these teachings illuminate about zeal?

The heart of true Christianity is nothing other than love coming to us on its way to someone else. This is God's design (or method) for the church—not to indoctrinate or create systems for "us against them," or what Wesley calls "pharisaic holiness." We are called to a different kind of zeal. Review what is said about this calling through a Wesleyan lens.

3. What are the characteristics of a zeal that can be harmful and destructive? What does misguided zeal look like?

Through this sermon, Wesley shows us what can happen when our zeal is misguided. It can bring much harm. We can be patient when we trust that God is at work, even in those who may see things differently than we do. In this same way, we can be kind. Zeal is akin to "soft" and the opposite of "hardness of heart." In love, we avoid "hard thoughts" towards others.

ADVENT, CHRISTMAS AND EPIPHANY

4. Explore or draw the concentric circles outlined in this chapter, placing the various dimensions of religion in proper connection to one another. What happens when we get these out of order? What are the possible fruits when we are able to live in this alignment as a community of faith?

Through the years, many have found this model to be helpful to communities wanting to grow in faithfulness and fruitfulness. We move from God's love to holy tempers (to use Wesley's language), to works of mercy, works of piety, and all the diverse gifts and perspectives of individuals within the body of Christ. How might this model be helpful to you and your community of faith?

5. Reflecting on the sermon for Christmas in this chapter, what is the relationship between love and blessing, both received and given? What does the image of blessing teach us about true and holy zeal?

The word "bless" comes from the root word meaning "to bend or bow." Christmas reveals God on bended knee, coming down to us and saying, "I love you." How might we receive this blessing? What are the implications of this blessing for how we live? What does this image teach us about true and holy zeal?

65

CHAPTER SIX

"The Unity of the Divine Being"

(A devotional paraphrase)

Sermon 114 in The Sermons of John Wesley

Then the scribe said to him, "You are right, Teacher; you have truly said that 'he is one, and besides him there is no other'; and 'to love him with all the heart, and with all the understanding, and with all the strength,' and 'to love one's neighbor as oneself,'—this is much more important than all whole burnt offerings and sacrifices."

Mark 12:32-33

Paraphrase of Wesley sermon

There is one God, one religion, and one happiness for all. There can't be more. Yet, in another sense, as the Apostle Paul observes, "There are many gods and many lords." In fact, the more polished we are, the more gods we tend to pile up. But to all who are favored with the Christian revelation, there is only one God.

But who can fully know this God? No one. We can only know what God is pleased to reveal. In light of the revelation we have received, some keywords are used to describe God. God is eternal, from everlasting to everlasting. Who can comprehend this? God is the One who was and is and is to come. God is omnipresent, existing in infinite space and time. God fills the heavens and the earth. God is omnipotent, with no bounds to power and presence. With God, "all things are possible." These attributes of God are more than the human heart can conceive. In the words of James, we read that all works are known to God, from every creature, from the beginning of the world, and even more, "from eternity." God knows the end and purpose of everything that exists.

"Holiness" is a key term used to describe the nature and character of God that has come to light for us through God's revealed word. Throughout scripture, this holiness is characterized by justice, trust, patience, and, above all, mercy. In a beautiful passage, we read where Moses says, "I beseech you, show me your glory." And the Lord descended in the cloud and proclaimed the name of God. God says, "I am the Lord." And then, a definition is given: "The Lord is merciful and gracious, slow to anger, and abounding in steadfast love, faithfulness, and forgiveness" (Exodus 34:5-6). This master text illuminates the way of true holiness.

God is Spirit, without parts or passions like we have, separate from all matter, and able to call into being all that is. This God created us in God's own image to be a reflection of eternal holiness. The outcome of this holiness is happiness. God made all things to be happy, happy in God. The saying of the ancient fathers is true: "Thou has made us for thyself, and our heart cannot rest till it finds rest in thee." This observation clearly answers the question, "For what purpose did God create humankind?" The answer is "To glorify and enjoy God forever." We can say it, but do we understand it? This core principle needs to be planted in every soul: "You are made to be happy in God." Every child needs to know this. We cannot teach this too soon.

We may think about being happy with God in heaven, but being happy with God on earth may not enter our minds. Such thoughts are hard when we are surrounded by idols promising a happiness independent from God. These idols, these rivals of God, are innumerable. They include objects promising to gratify the desires of our sinful imaginations and our love of the world. These idols always leave us wanting.

This danger is found in religion as well. Any religion that does not imply the giving of our hearts to God is a false religion. It is tempting, for example, to focus on a religion of opinions, which we call orthodoxy. Many of us fall into this snare, professing to hold "salvation by grace through faith," but by "faith" only mean a system of Arminian or Calvinist opinions. This snare also happens with "religion of forms," of outward rituals and styles. We can also turn these outward rituals into idols, where they block the love of God rather than open us to it. We can fall into this same trap with "religion of works," where we seek the favor of God by doing good or judging others. With any of these as the focus, our worship will leave us short of the joy God wants for us.

True religion is having the right temperament towards God and Creation. That temperament is one of gratitude and goodwill. It is gratitude to God that leads us to goodwill to others. Love of God opens the way for us to love our neighbor as a part of ourselves. This is at the heart of true religion. We cannot emphasize this too much. From this heart of religion flows the happiness for which we were made. We are happy first in the consciousness of God's favor, which indeed is better than life itself. Next, we are happy in our constant communion with the Father and Jesus Christ. Then, we are happy in all the heavenly tempers given by the Holy Spirit, by which our happiness increases as we mature into the "measure of the full stature of Christ" (Eph 4:13).

But how little is this religion experienced? We need to hear the lamentation of a dying saint, Mr. Haliburton of St. Andrew's in Scotland, who said: "I am afraid a kind of rational religion is more and more prevailing among us; a religion that has nothing of Christ belonging to it … even among those who call themselves Christians." We live in a time when many people focus on our duty to neighbor as the essence of religion and forget about our relationship with God. Philosophers like Rousseau, Voltaire, and Hume have extolled humanity to the skies as the essence of religion, sparing no pains to establish a religion that should stand on its own foundation, independent of any revelation.

It is no wonder that this religion should grow fashionable. But call it humanity, virtue, morality, or what you please; it is neither better nor worse than atheism. This religion puts "asunder what God has joined": the love of God with the love of neighbor. We cannot thrust God out of the world that God has made, perhaps believing that "since he gave things their beginning, and set this whirligig a-spinning, he had not concerned himself with these trifles, but let everything take its own course." On the contrary, we have the fullest evidence that the eternal, omnipresent, omnipotent, all-wise Spirit continually superintends whatever is created. God governs from everlasting to everlasting. Whoever teaches happiness without God is a monster and the pest of society.

We know by scripture and experience that true happiness cannot be found until we discover that sin is the root of all misery and that the mercy of God is the remedy. By the blood of Jesus, we are redeemed or "brought back" into a relationship with God. By the Holy Spirit, the love of God is then "shed abroad in our hearts" (Rom 5:5). By this love, we are transformed into humble, gentle, patient witnesses to the ways of God, always thankful in every step for God's abiding providence. This is true holiness. This is true happiness. The goodwill or benevolence that springs from this relationship is what we can call true religion.

Therefore, make it your desire to walk in the path of God's love. Beware of anyone who takes only half of religion for the whole. Love God and love neighbor as yourself. Put no other rule before this one, and no other gods before this God, who is not only the Creator but also the Redeemer, Sustainer, Preserver, Sanctifier, Comforter, Savior, Lord, and Friend. From God's fountain, let every action and affection flow in gratitude and goodwill.

Amen.

"The Wisest Gift of the Magi"

2 Corinthians 5:16-21 and Matthew 2:1-12

One gift the wise men brought to the Christ child exceeded all others in value. One gift. Which one?[10] Was it the frankincense? I suppose if you conflate Matthew's birth story with Luke's, put them together, and picture the wise men arriving at the stable, as most of our nativity scenes do, then you might think no gift was worth more than frankincense. Frankincense would have masked the odors of the barn. It would make visitors feel welcome. That's what frankincense was for.

But in truth, although centuries of Christian art have featured shepherds and wise men all together at the stable, Matthew knows nothing of a stable or shepherds. Matthew has the holy family in a house, and no shepherds or animals are mentioned when the wise men arrive. In fact, some scholars believe that Matthew envisions this meeting taking place months, if not years, after the birth. Jesus was a boy, not a baby, at this time. So, frankincense would not have been needed immediately.

What about myrrh? Myrrh was a type of oil used to anoint kings and anoint persons for special missions. That certainly tells us something about Jesus, even as a child. The title "Christ" literally means "anointed one," or one who represents God and brings God to us. Myrrh was also the oil used to prepare bodies for burial. You may remember the story of the woman at Bethany who poured costly ointment over Jesus. The disciples criticized her, but Jesus praised her, saying, "She has prepared me for burial." Thus, this gift of ointment reminds us that this child would come face to face with death and conquer it. He is anointed to give life to us all. So, as this gift of myrrh represents that anointment, it is still not the gift I believe is the most important.

So, that leaves gold, right? Money is always needed. At that time, it would have come in handy for them, perhaps to secure this child's future and help him get started in ministry. But how much value would gold be to one who trusted totally in God? Would gold be at the top of the list for the one who would say that Solomon, in all his glory, was not arrayed as splendidly as a single lily of the field? No, Jesus was not concerned with accumulating wealth.

So which gift was the most valuable—frankincense, myrrh, gold—or perhaps the other gift mentioned three times in this scripture? Maybe you missed it. It is the gift that is central to the story, the gift of "worship." As I said, it was mentioned three times. First, early in the story, these wise ones acknowledge that they undertook their journey specifically to worship a new king. Worship was important to them. Some translations say, "pay homage," which means "to kneel," "to adore," "to declare worth," or "to worship." Secondly, Herod tried to con them by saying he, too, wanted to worship this new king. Of course, this was the one thing he needed to do, but he had no real intention of doing it. Then, at the end of this part of the story, the Magi arrived after a long journey, and they "kneeled down and worshiped him."

An important theological point must be made as we start a new year. Jesus Christ is worthy of our worship. John

Wesley makes this clear in the sermon we are using in this chapter to inspire us. And although Wesley does not use the Magi as an illustration, we can. These wise ones gazed upon the Christ child and knew deep within that he was not to be regarded from "a human point of view." He would be more than a teacher to be respected and followed. He would be more than a prophet inspired by God. The wise men were able to look at this child and see Emmanuel, "God with us." They were able to look at him and see God's power to give eternal life. And so, they worshiped him. And this worship changed them. It changed the very direction of their lives. We are told they went home by another way. They did not go back to Herod. They lived in a way that would allow the love of Christ to come into the world.

To worship Christ means we can no longer separate the divine and the human, with God "up-there" and us "down-here," keeping God at a distance so we can go about our business as if nothing has changed. To worship Christ means we cannot continue in our divisive and self-centered ways, dividing even God from us. For God, in Christ, has reconciled us together, not counting our sins against us, as our first scripture reading reminded us. In Christ, God has come all the way into our lives, into our joy, into our sorrows, into our lives, and into our death, able to redeem it all. Yes, Jesus Christ is worthy of our worship.

In our first scripture in this lesson, the Apostle Paul cautions us against regarding Christ from a "human point of view." We can be too casual in our view of Christ. We might think of Jesus as a friend we need to keep in touch with occasionally or as a buddy who will not let us down no matter what. There is some truth in that, but this casual perspective allows us to forget or ignore that we are in the presence of the most-high God incarnate in the world. We stand before the One whom the angels approached with "speechless awe." Jesus is more than a cute baby, a kind man, or a good teacher. We are not to regard him from a human point of view. Jesus Christ is worthy of our worship.

There is a moral implication to our worship of Christ. When we worship Christ, we are moved beyond our human point of view when it comes to how we regard each other as well. We are lifted up to a higher perspective, able to see beyond country, color, status, or even sin. Through Christ our Lord, we are reconciled to God without any of "this" getting in the way, and being reconciled to God, we are able to see each other as worthy of the same love we have received. Yes, Christ is worthy of our worship because, through him, we become a part of something much bigger than ourselves. We are included into God's eternal love.

As we enter a new year, I invite you to make worship a priority. Take time to bow down to the holy and bring this holiness into your life. Be reconciled to God through Christ, and through Christ, be an instrument of God's reconciling love, forgiveness, and grace in the world. Let us all enter this new year remembering the carol's words, "O come let us adore him, Christ the Lord."

Amen.

Reflections for Personal Devotion and Discipling

1. What is theology, and why is it important?

Wesley did not write a systematic theology. For him, theology was a thoughtful reflection on Christian worship and living. To this end, his theology took the form of sermons, prayers, letters, and hymns. This type of theology has been called "Practical Divinity."[11] It develops and grows and thus is subject to change and evolution. In another place, Wesley uses the phrase "patience with contradictions." We need this because we are fallible and finite, all with different gifts and perspectives and at different places on our faith journey. Impatience with contradictions comes when we equate faith with "orthodoxy" or "right opinion." Wesley consistently says that this understanding of faith blocks the way of love and our opportunities to truly glorify God.

2. How do you describe God? What is the difference between describing God in terms of a philosophical concept or in terms of character?

In describing God, we can learn a lot from words like eternal, omnipresence, and omnipotent. Yet, this description can serve to keep God in the abstract. It can be more than the human heart can conceive. From the scriptures, we see God described more often in terms of character, and "holiness" is a word that sums up God's character. God's holiness is revealed through attributes of justice, trust, patience, and mercy, to name a few. In Christ, God's character becomes incarnate in the world. Through his life, death, and resurrection, we know God and what God wants for us. We are called to reflect this same holiness in our lives. We are invited into a relationship where this becomes possible.

3. What can we do to focus our worship on the one true God?
Why is it important to have only one God?

Holiness leads to happiness in this life. The biggest obstacle to this happiness is the worship of other "gods." And as Wesley says, the more "polished" we are, the more gods we tend to pile up, trusting in them to bring happiness they promise but can't deliver. We divide God by our own prejudices and desires, and we then become divided. The hope of God is that our lives will be unified into God's whole and perfect love. The hope is that healing will come to our broken and divided beings.

4. Revisit the notion of true religion. How is true religion defined? What are the dangers in defining it in terms of doctrines or practices?

Putting our faith in religious opinion, orthodoxy, outward rituals, or styles brings division to the church and our own hearts. When we champion our own finite opinions about what is "right" for all, we limit God to our understanding and thus fail to see the whole of God's love. Over and over again, Wesley makes it clear that true religion is not found in our opinions or particular understandings. As he says in another place, all this is "quite wide of the point." True religion is rooted in love. In this sermon, Wesley says true religion can be characterized by these two words: gratitude and goodwill. How do these words illuminate what God wants for us and from us?

More Than...

The Season of Epiphany

God wants more for us and from us, and we are challenged to do more than settle. As inspiration for this series, we will use Wesley's first eight sermons in his standard sermons for the church. There is a reason why these sermons are first. They provide foundational teachings to guide on the way of salvation.

CHAPTER SEVEN

"Salvation by Faith"

(A devotional paraphrase)

Sermon 1 in The Standard Sermons of John Wesley

"By grace you are saved through faith."

Paraphrase of Wesley sermon

For anyone exploring the Christian faith, perhaps the best place to start is with the concept of grace. Grace is at the heart of it all, pumping life into all dimensions of our lives—moral, emotional, relational, theological, personal, and organizational. Grace binds it all together.

So, what is this grace? The Greek word *charis* simply means "gift." We get the word "charity" from this Greek root. Biblically, however, this common word describes a very special gift. Grace is the free, undeserved, unearned, amazing favor of God. Grace is God looking at you and saying, "Oh, how much I love you and want so much for you."

In its most complete way, this grace is revealed to the world through the life, death, and resurrection of Jesus Christ. Christ is God's grace. In Christ, we receive "grace upon grace" (John 1:16). Our response can be summed up with these words, "Thanks be to God for this unspeakable gift" (2 Cor 9:15).

How does grace affect us? What changes occur in the light of grace? By grace, God embraces our darkness and dread with a light that leads us into forgiveness and love. By grace, God embraces our pain with compassion, leading us into true joy. By grace, God embraces our doubt with such patience and gentleness that we are able to move from fear to faith. And—this is so big—by grace, we are able to reclaim ourselves as created in the image of God.

So now we turn to the word "faith." What is faith? Faith is more than "believing that ..." Even the devil believes "that" God exists and "that" Jesus is the Son of God (Luke 9:34, James 2:19). Faith is much more than believing and much more than a cold, lifeless assent to a creed or doctrine. Faith is trust springing up from the heart. It is trusting not in our own merits or opinions but in the merits of the life, death, and resurrection of Jesus Christ, the one whose death opened the way to eternal life for all.

So, now we turn to the word "salvation." What is salvation? The word "salvation" means to be made whole, one with God, one with each other, one in ministry to all the world. By grace, we have been "made whole" in our relationship with God. By grace, we are being saved, even now. Whatever else salvation implies, the first thing to be said is that it is a present gift. Right now, we are delivered from sin. In this world, we are set free from the fear that accompanies sin. We are set free from the chains of our guilt, our anger, our greed, our lust, our envy, our arrogance, all that might hold us back from entering into God's life-giving love (see 1 Cor 1:18, 15:2; Phil 2:12-13; 1 Pet 2:2).

The first usual objection when preaching about salvation by grace through faith is that we are preaching against holiness and good works. This might be true if the proclaimer believes faith is somehow separate from holiness. We, however, do not proclaim that. Faith is not separate from holiness or good works; rather, "our salvation produces good works" (Eph 2:10). Faith "responds" by striving to live by the virtues of Christ and bearing the fruit of the Spirit. Faith produces this desire within us.

Another objection is that preaching faith leads people into spiritual arrogance, as if they are able to know or receive something that others don't know or haven't received. This might happen out of our ignorance, but it is not intended. Anytime we boast or lift up our righteous opinions to set ourselves apart from others, we are not giving witness to God's gracious salvation. If we boast in anything, our boasting is to be in the richness of God's mercy as God saves us by grace, even when we are dead in sin. Our boasting before others should only be to say that God loves them.

By focusing on grace rather than works, are we encouraging people to sin? "God is gracious, so what does it matter?" some might claim. Indeed, this is possible. But this is not the purpose. True grace leads to repentance, or the turning to God. As we turn away from our selfish focus and turn into God's expansive love, our hearts open up to God's will, and our lives grow in the virtues of true holiness, exemplified in the fruits of the Spirit: love, joy, peace, patience, kindness, goodness, gentleness, faithfulness, and temperance (Gal 5:22). We grow in such practices of grace not to earn God's favor but in response to it. In fact, we cannot trust Christ's merits until we renounce our own merits in humility and with a desire for mercy. Those who try to establish their own righteousness cannot receive the righteousness of God.

This is the reason for grace. We are sinners. We fall short of the glory of God. We can never measure up to the standards of holiness. Apart from grace, our righteousness always becomes self-righteousness. In trying to justify ourselves before God, we only bring God down to our level and thus sin even more. If salvation depends on our efforts to measure up, we are all doomed. And so God comes in grace, the very heart of the Christian message.

We proclaim God's mercy is for all. It is for the likes of Zacchaeus, a public thief, Mary Magdalene, a common prostitute, or the person you resent, abhor, or judge! Grace calls us to look at the log in our own eye before we worry about the speck in the eye of another. Grace leads us to say, "Even I may hope for this mercy; it is there for even me" (we are indebted to Martin Luther for reminding us of this).

Don't let any adversary, worldly or spiritual, stand in the way of life for you. You are invited to turn to God and believe in your heart that God's grace is able to lead you out of sin und lead you into a life of virtue, all by way of the cross where all debts were paid and the way to life was opened. You are invited into a grace able to swallow up death itself, all for you.

Is God calling you to this grace? If so, then you are invited, wherever you are, to profess Christ as your Savior and be among those who say: "Thanks be to God, who gives us victory through our Lord Jesus Christ, to whom, with the Father and the Holy Spirit, be blessings, and glory, and wisdom, and honor, and power, and might, forever and ever. Amen."

"More Than...a Ticket to Heaven"

Luke 19:1-10 and Ephesians 2:1-10

A million-dollar bill was handed to me in a restaurant a few weeks ago. It poses the million-dollar question on the back: "Are you saved? If you died today, would you go to heaven?" And then, there are a couple of paragraphs intended to scare one into salvation. I admire the woman who gave it to me. She had concern for my soul. But I also want you to know that, if not flawed, her concern was incomplete from our Wesleyan understanding of salvation.

Many people in our culture see "being saved" as a judicial or legal term indicating that when one receives Jesus into their heart, their name is written in the Book of Life. In short, salvation is viewed as a "ticket to heaven" or a "get out of hell free" card. We get this "ticket" when WE make certain claims about what WE believe, and if WE say the right words with enough sincerity, then WE are saved. This is a prominent understanding of salvation in our culture. And I want to be clear: parts of this understanding are important. Salvation does include the assurance of eternal life. It does connect us to heaven. But, from a Wesleyan perspective, there is much more to it.

The word "salvation" means to be "made whole," to be reconciled, healed, or made one with God, one with each other, and one in ministry to all the world. We pray these words regularly when we call upon the Holy Spirit to bless the bread and cup. Salvation is being brought back into God's presence and God's love even now.

Without this relationship, we are lost. It is not so much that we are "bad," as some assume. It is that we are lost—lost in the fear of living and the dread of dying, lost in our attempts to play God and fix things we cannot fix, lost in anger and envy, greed, and lust that can bring so much harm into the world. How did Jesus respond to this lostness? He said, "I have compassion upon them, for they are like sheep without a shepherd" (Mark 6:34). Jesus came to seek and save the lost (Luke 19:10).

The story of Zacchaeus provides a great illustration. Jesus said to him, "Today salvation has come to this house." At that moment, Zacchaeus' life was changed. He was transformed from focusing on money to focusing on relationships; he was transformed from valuing his position in society to using his gifts to connect with others. In this relationship with Jesus, Zacchaeus found true joy and true life. That's salvation.

It is worth noting how others grumbled and complained about Jesus choosing this man, this sinner, and wanting to eat with him. Why would Jesus want to be with him rather than them? That's a bad trap to fall into, which leads us to this notion of grace.

As Paul says, "For by grace you have been saved through faith, and this is not your own doing, it is a gift of God—not the result of works, so that no one may boast." The word "grace" simply means "gift." That's how salvation is given—as a gift. We don't earn this blessing in any way. In fact, any attempt to earn it or prove to God how good we are just brings God down to our level and tells God that salvation is not about grace, that it is about reward and us proving that we are worthy, and it is about dividing the world into the good and the bad, us and them. If we see salvation through this lens, then we will be among those who have trouble with Jesus hanging out with Zacchaeus. Why would Jesus want to waste his time with that guy when he could hang out with us? This popular "religious" perspective actually blinds us to true religion.

Bono, the leader of the group U2, once had this to say about "being saved." He said, "You see, at the center of many religions is the idea of Karma. You know, what you put out comes back to you; an eye for an eye, a tooth for a tooth ... But then, along comes this idea called 'grace' to upend all that 'as you reap, so you will sow' stuff ... in my case (he says) this is very good news because I've done a lot of stupid stuff ... I'd be in big trouble if Karma was going to be my judge ... I'm holding out for Grace ... I don't have to depend on my own religiosity."[12]

Paul says, "You are saved by grace through FAITH" (and if you read the paraphrase of Wesley's first sermon in his Standard Sermons, these are the words he deals with: salvation, grace, and faith). Let us now reflect on what faith is and is not.

Faith is more than affirming certain creeds or doctrines. As James says in his letter, even demons believe that Jesus is God's son or that God exists. Just affirming doctrines or saying you believe is not the kind of faith God wants for us. Faith is also more than trusting in Jesus and making a commitment to follow him, although that is an important part of it. But before this happens, faith is a gift. Trust comes after God, by grace, moves in our lives. Faith is a divine conviction, a God-given knowing deep in our hearts that God is with us and God loves us, forgives us, transforms us, and is there to see us through even death itself. Faith is the giving of our lives to this grace. This faith comes through Jesus, and it changes everything.

It happened for Zacchaeus. Through his guilt, greed, and all that might have caused him to resist, God's love came in, and with a deep "knowing," his life was changed. Jesus described this as "salvation coming to him."

Here's the way it works. Grace leads us to faith, which then leads us into "true holiness" or "true religion." And to review, once again, "true religion," through our Wesleyan lens, is not rooted in doctrines or creeds or anything that pits us against others. True religion is rooted in a relationship with God that yields love, joy, and peace and helps us to be more patient, kind, and gentle. Through these virtues and blessings, we are "being saved," as the scripture says, and able to "grow *in* salvation"—not just *towards* salvation as if it is only there when we die, but it is *in* salvation right now (see 1 Cor 1:18, 15:2; 1 Pet 2:2).[13]

So, even now, you are invited into a grace that can lead you out of darkness and into light. You are invited into a grace able to swallow up death itself. I invite you to examine your own heart. Is God calling you to this grace? Another way to ask it is, "Are you being saved?"

Amen.

Reflections for Personal Devotion and Discipling

1. When you hear the question, "Are you saved?" what emotions or feelings are evoked within you?

   Fear, relief, apprehension, anger, doubt, assurance, hope, joy—what experiences are behind this response? How has John Wesley's sermon "Salvation by Faith" and our use of this theme changed your response or given you a new way to think about salvation?

2. How does the lens we use to view salvation determine how we interact with one another?

   If we think of salvation as something to be earned in order to receive our ticket to heaven, then it becomes a deal between an individual and God. Salvation is only concerned with what happens to us in the afterlife. If you aren't saved, you can't go to heaven. In contrast, how does our interaction with others change if salvation is attainable in the present, as John Wesley indicates? Salvation calls us into right relationship with God in the present and in eternal life and calls us to seek ways to be in right relationship with all of God's people. Wesley believed this "salvation by grace through faith" was available for all. This means grace and mercy are for all. How does this change the way we interact with others?

3. What are we saved "from"? What are we saved "for"?

   John Wesley focused on both dimensions of salvation. You are invited to reflect and engage in conversation about it. How does this gift change our lives in the present?

4. Is God calling you to this grace?

   The Wesleyan way is for us to spend time every day examining our spiritual lives, receiving God's gifts, and striving to grow in these gifts. Grace leads us to faith, which leads us into "true holiness." What resources are available to help us along this life-giving way?

CHAPTER EIGHT

"The Almost Christian"

(A devotional paraphrase)

Sermon 2 in The Standard Sermons of John Wesley

"Almost thou persuadest me to be a Christian."

Acts 26:28

Paraphrase of Wesley sermon

So many go right to the edge and are almost fully committed Christians. Many, however, stop at the "don'ts"— don't steal, don't cheat, don't lie, don't oppress the poor. Faith in this regard is equated with what we are *not* to do. The temptation is to think this is enough when, in fact, it is nothing more than common decency for believers and nonbelievers alike.

Many go beyond the negative and actually try to do good— when it is convenient. They may feed the hungry if they have food to spare or provide clothing with their hand-me-downs, making room in their closets for more. In this regard, it is easy to justify such acts as good and faithful. Many set the bar of faith here. This bar of faith is easy to achieve and is at the base level of being an "almost Christian."

Being "almost Christian" might entail following outward

forms of faith initially expressed in the negative. In this situation, we try not to curse or take God's name in vain. We avoid obvious uncleanliness, gossip, slander, and the like. We may even abstain from excess wine, gluttony, strife, and contention and endeavor to live peaceably with others.

Many, out of a desire for meaning and purpose, go far beyond "cheap and easy acts of kindness." With great courage, they engage in good works—comforting the afflicted, teaching those who need help, and providing for those in need. In such acts, we see forms of godliness that we can graciously affirm and encourage. Living this way is an important part of the journey to being more than an "almost Christian."

Some, at this place on the journey, are also committed to the "means of grace"—worship, prayer, fellowship, and service—and they engage in these practices not just for "show," as some do, those who are "loaded with gold and costly apparel." No, the "almost Christian" approaches faith with much more seriousness and attention. They are sincere, devoted, and genuinely desire to serve God and lift others up.

But here is the question. Is it possible to go so far as this and still be an "almost Christian?" Another way to ask is, What more is implied in being an "altogether Christian?" First and foremost, the altogether or complete Christian is filled with God's love—in heart, soul, mind, and will. In this love, our desire is for God, not for the things of this world. In this love, all forms of arrogance and selfish gain have been crucified with Christ, and we have been raised as new creations in Christ (Mark 12:29-31, 2 Cor 5:17).

Secondly, for an altogether Christian, this love of God

planted deep within, springs up into love of neighbor. If anyone asks, "Who is my neighbor," the heartfelt reply is "everyone." We want to love as Christ loves us. This love is patient and kind. It is not rash or hasty in judging. It is not "puffed up" with pride and knowing all the answers. It seeks not its own will "but only the good of others, that they may be saved." The altogether Christian knows that God's love always comes to us on its way to someone else (see 1 Cor 13:4-8).

Finally, although not separate from this love, is faith. This faith is more than believing, understanding that even the devil believes. The right and true Christian faith is more than believing that the Holy Scriptures and the Articles of Faith are true. At its core, Christian faith embodies a sure trust and confidence that our sins are forgiven by the merits of Christ, that we are reconciled to God's favor, and that this faith leads us into love. This faith is a gift that "purifies our hearts" and fills us with a love stronger than death. In trust, we give our lives to this love after we have received it as a gift. To be clear, a faith that does not lead to love is "a dead and devilish one."

Our scripture shows the Apostle Paul in chains before King Agrippa. Even in this circumstance, he proclaims the gospel. The king says, "You are almost persuading me to become a Christian" (Acts 26:28). That is Paul's hope, but Paul can't do this for him. Only the Holy Spirit can make this connection. Like Paul, we can give testimony and show the way. We can spark this movement of the Spirit with needed self-examination: Do I abstain from evil? Do I try to be good? Do I sincerely desire to serve God? Whether you have gotten this far or not, the Holy Spirit is there to help you overcome your fear and give you this desire to devote all your words and works to God's glory and to live fully in God's love.

Deep within, do you want this? Do you desire to be truly happy and able to rejoice in the life God has given you, knowing that this life is a part of something so much bigger—even eternally bigger? Can you envision the possibility of this love springing up from the depths of your soul to be shared with everyone you meet—even your enemies and those perceived to be enemies of God? Will you open your heart to God's forgiveness given to you through Christ's redemptive sacrifice on the cross, where Christ took away our sins, cast them into the sea, and opened the door to new life for you? Do you want to live in relationship with the One who shines the light that overcomes all forms of darkness and death? One more question: Do you know that the Holy Spirit is bearing witness with your spirit even now, as you are indeed a child of God?

May these questions awaken you who are spiritually asleep. Call on your Savior while you have breath. The Lord, who is merciful and gracious, abounding in steadfast love, forgiving all sin, is there for you and calling for you. Don't stop short of this high calling. Don't stop at "almost" embracing it. May we all experience what it is to be, not "almost" only but "altogether" a child of God and follower of the One who brings redemption, peace, and life. As we leap into these gifts, the love of God comes pouring out into our beings and through us to the world. That's God's method for our salvation and the salvation of the world. Amen.

"More Than...Almost"

Acts 26:24-32

You may have heard the saying, "Almost only counts in horseshoes and hand grenades." That saying assumes that "almost" is not good enough, which is true in many situations. If you are flying, you don't want the pilot to "almost" land on the runway. If you are running a race, you don't want to "almost" cross the finish line.

Sometimes, however, the word "almost" is more positive and can spark hope and excitement. We might think of scientists on the brink of a new discovery. After years of research, they are almost there. Or think of a student who is almost finished and ready to graduate. Or think of being on a road trip when a child asks for the twentieth time, "Are we there yet?" and you can truly say, "Almost." It can be an encouraging word.

This more positive take on "almost" gives us a better understanding of what it means to be an "Almost Christian." That's the title of John Wesley's second sermon in his Standard Sermons. What qualifies as an "Almost Christian?"

Theologian Kenda Creasy Dean recently wrote a book with the same title, *Almost Christian*, and a phrase she uses to describe many Christians in the United States is "Moralistic Therapeutic Deism." This type of Christianity uses the language of the faith but focuses too much on the self. The focus is on being nice and feeling good about yourself, with a vague idea that a deity is there to help us succeed. This may be the most popular form of religion

95

in the United States, and many churches thrive on it. To be a little more challenging, Kenda Dean says that Moral Therapeutic Deism is a watered-down version of the gospel. It is a self-centered version of the gospel that focuses on self-preservation rather than self-giving love. It misses the sense that we are called to go out and be a light to the world, to give hope and healing, and perhaps even to suffer on behalf of others. In other words, Moral Therapeutic Deism is "Almost Christian."

So how do we move from "almost" to "fully" Christian, or as Wesley calls it, an "altogether" Christian? According to this book, there are four characteristics of what Dean calls "consequential faith," or a faith that truly shapes how we live:

1. Being able to articulate beliefs in a heartfelt and personal way.

2. Being a part of a community of faith where people discuss issues of faith and life.

3. Having a sense of God's calling to live on behalf of others rather than self.

4. An understanding that we are part of something bigger than ourselves, that our lives are caught up in a larger story that is going somewhere because it is guided by God.[14]

When I read these characteristics, my first thought was the "Brag on Jesus" retreat our mid-youth went on. Without doing it directly, they focused on these characteristics, and at one point, while talking about how to articulate their faith, the youth were struggling with what to say. And then a couple of them, at the same time, started saying the Apostle's

Creed. In that moment, they "got it." They had a resource planted in their heart to help them talk about their faith in a personal way. And they could do this because of what happens in worship every week.

In his sermon "Almost Christian," John Wesley gives us a personal testimony of how he once found himself in the "almost" stage. In this stage, he worked hard at being good, but it was still mostly about wanting to feel good about himself. Wesley was highly committed to the practices of faith—worship, prayer, and service. He studied scripture and doctrine, but it felt more like drudgery than life-giving. In his sermon, he sympathizes with all who get stuck in "almost," and he wanted them—and he wants us—to know the answer on how to move from "almost" to being an "altogether" Christian. The answer is "love"—that's actually Wesley's answer to many questions of faith. God wants this for us: love, love filling our whole being—heart, soul, mind, and will. In this love, all forms of selfishness fade away. In this love, we grow in patience and kindness. We stop judging others. Our practice of faith becomes life-giving and purposeful. That's what happens when God's love enters our hearts.

This love is at the heart of true religion. Now, get this. True religion is not rooted in doctrine, creed, or style of worship or, as Wesley says, "anything external to the heart." Faith is rooted in the heart and in a love that is even able to conquer death itself. If that's true religion, then false religion is when we get hung up on practices, doctrines, and judgments and start using "religion" to divide us up and pit ourselves against one another. Doctrines, creeds, and practices are important, but they are resources for faith, not the focus of faith. When we make them our focus and believe that faith is about defending them, religion can become a destructive force.

So, you are invited to engage in your own self-examination. In a true Wesleyan spirit, we must say that nobody else can do this for you. This is between you and God. It is the job of the church to provide support and guidance, but the church can't take the place of a relationship with God through Jesus Christ. We can only point you to that relationship. In our scripture lesson, we see Paul in chains, standing before a king proclaiming the good news. He tells the king of his conversion and missionary journeys, and at one point, King Agrippa says, "You are almost persuading me to become a Christian" (using Wesley's translation). Here "almost" implies that he just might come to a personal relationship with Christ, as so many have. That is Paul's hope, but Paul can't do this for him. Only the Holy Spirit can make this connection.

John Wesley loved questions to help spark this connection. Here are a few questions that might help you connect to God's work at a heart level: Do you desire to be truly happy and able to live knowing that your life is a part of something so much bigger than yourself? Can you envision the possibility of this love springing up from the depths of your soul to be shared with everyone you meet? Do you want to live in relationship with the One who shines the light that can overcome all forms of darkness and death?

Here's the call: Don't stop at "almost." Don't stop short of the high calling to which you are being summoned. May you experience what it means to be more than "almost," to be "altogether," a child of God and follower of Jesus Christ, God's son, the One who brings redemption and peace and opens the way of life, the One who did not stop at "almost" but gave his all.

Amen.

Reflections for Personal Devotion and Discipling

1. What motivates an "altogether Christian?"

In this sermon, Wesley differentiates between an "almost Christian" and an "altogether Christian." While being an "almost Christian" doesn't seem like such a bad thing, Wesley highlights one major difference between the two distinctions: why they desire to do good. One does so with a focus on self, the other as a grateful response to God's life-giving love. Take some time to reflect upon what motivates an "almost Christian" and what motivates an "altogether Christian."

2. Are you fully alive, experiencing the love of God in your heart and overflowing from it?

We have defined "true religion" as a relationship with God, and it is not rooted in certain practices or doctrines. An "almost Christian" believes the means, practices, and doctrines are the end or purpose. But for Wesley, an "altogether Christian" understands that the practices we hold dear and the doctrines we profess are a means to the end, which is to experience the love of God. When we understand this, we allow God's love to dwell in our lives, and we become fully alive. Are you fully alive, experiencing the love of God in your heart and overflowing from it, or are you temporarily happy because of the practices you're committed to and the creeds you can recite? What are the negative consequences when we confuse the end with the means?

3. Have you had a transforming moment when you felt the Holy Spirit calling you to move from an "almost Christian" to an "altogether Christian"?

In the first half of his sermon, Wesley gives examples of how other people act as "almost Christians" rather than "altogether Christians." He talks about people exhibiting outward religion and being driven by fear of sin or "love of virtue." But all of a sudden, the examples of an "almost Christian" shift from other people to himself. He gives his own testimony. Thus, his sermon is not a rebuke of other Christians

100

but, instead, a reflection of who he has been and how the love of God and love of neighbor transformed his life. Have you had a transforming moment when you felt the Holy Spirit calling you to move from an "almost Christian" to an "altogether Christian?"

CHAPTER NINE

"Awake Thou that Sleepest"
(A devotional paraphrase)

Sermon 3 in The Standard Sermons of John Wesley,
written by Charles Wesley

*"Sleeper awake! Rise from the dead,
and Christ will shine on you."*

Ephesians 5:14

Paraphrase of Wesley sermon

Our natural state of existence could be described as a deep sleep of the soul. In this spiritual slumber, we see no need for the one thing needful: that inward transformation, the sanctification of spirit and body, without which we cannot see the Lord. In this state, we can know so much about the world. We can consume ourselves with trivia and trash but know so little about ourselves. We do not know that our only business in this world is to regain that image of God in which we were created.

In this darkness of spiritual night, we can fantasize that we are in perfect health while full of disease. Bound in misery, we can think we are free. We can believe we are at peace, even as the pit of hell opens its mouth to swallow us up. We hear no alarm to "flee from the wrath to come." We do not cry out, "What must I do to be saved?"

103

And it must be noted that this sleep may be at its deepest when we move through life with a sense of our own goodness, always compared to others. In this state, we might find ourselves as zealous and orthodox as Pharisees who work hard to justify ourselves and establish our own righteousness. We cry out, "I'm glad I'm not like that guy. Lord, look at me." To use another scriptural image from Jesus, we may be like painted tombs, beautiful on the outside but full of dead bones with no breath of Spirit to give life.

Our Savior sounds the alarm and cries out: Awake! Arise from the dead! Stir yourself up and shake off the dust. In Acts, we read the story of Paul and Silas singing and praying in prison. When the Lord shakes loose the shackles, they have an opportunity to escape. Instead, they stay in the cell out of concern for the jailor watching them. In thanksgiving, this prison guard cries, "What must I do to be saved? To have this same peace? This same sense of the eternal? This same freedom from fear?" He is awakened to truth. His life and his family's life are transformed. This act of love opened his heart to hear the call.

This alarm can come in the form of soul-stirring questions: How is it with your soul? Have you secured the one necessary thing? Have you recovered the image of God and desire to live by true holiness? Have you cast off the old, put on the new, and clothed yourself with Christ? Have you received the Holy Spirit?

Do you know what true religion is? It is participation in the divine nature, the life of God in your soul, Christ formed in your heart. It is holiness and happiness, indeed heaven begun on earth. It is a kingdom of God within you.

It is not "meat or drink, or any outward thing. Instead, it is righteousness and peace and joy in the Holy Spirit. It is an everlasting kingdom planted within, bringing a peace that passes all human understanding."

I believe this is what all of us want deep within. In our fallen state, we try to save and justify ourselves. In our dreams of worldly happiness, we look for this salvation in dangerous places. But even here, there is a sign of hope, for we are stirring in our sleep. We all hope to be saved.

The story of the prodigal son is inspiring on many levels. Here is a son who leaves home with his inheritance to make it on his own. In his struggle to make it, the scripture says, "He came to himself" (Luke 15:17). He was awakened. He remembered home. He remembered that he was loved. And as he turned towards home, he discovered his father was not just waiting and watching but running to meet him. That's the promise for us as well. God has this same love for us. May we "come to ourselves" and be so awakened.

Our conscience bears witness deep within that God is there for us. Search inside and see if this is not so for you. God's gifts of eternal life and love are there for you. Deep within, the Spirit of truth dwells with you and in you (John 14:17). Search inside and see if this is true for you. Hear the alarm. May all who are spiritually asleep wake up.

Some deny this idea regarding the inspiration of the Spirit. They say that the Spirit comforts and assists perhaps but does not move us or stir within us. Our church knows nothing of this devilish distinction. Our church speaks of being moved by the Holy Spirit and prays for the inspiration of the Holy Spirit. We choose to listen to the "foolishness" of

God over the "wise" among us who ridicule this desire for inspiration and call it madness and enthusiasm. We don't want this apostasy to numb us to God's work within us and turn faith into something to be studied rather than lived.

Just look around! Our land mourns under the floods of ungodliness. What keeps our hearts from being pierced in the wake of such profaneness, blasphemies, lying, slandering, Sabbath-breaking, gluttony, drunkenness, revenge, adulteries, frauds, injustice, and extortion as such conditions spread over our land like a flood? There is a raging flood among us, fueled by our desires for luxury and self-indulgence, our thirst for praise and power, and our displays of righteousness where we become like painted tombs, shiny on the outside yet filled with fear and death on the inside, lacking in spiritual power.

Sisters and brothers, it is time to awaken out of this sleep. The great trumpet of the Lord blows. O may we speedily see the things that make for peace before they are hidden from our eyes. Stir up repentance within and awaken in us the principles of the Reformation, the truth and simplicity of the gospel. May the bones within come to life with the breath of your Holy Spirit. May the Holy Spirit bear witness with our spirits that we are children of God. Come Holy Spirit, awaken your church!

Amen.

More Than...Physically Awake

Isaiah 50:4-5 and Ephesians 5:8-14

The fire alarm went off at the church not long ago, and I want to tell you my first thought. Since it had happened before, my first thought was to ignore it. I thought, "It's probably nothing." So, I continued to work. Then suddenly, I remembered an article I read years ago about the danger of ignoring alarms in buildings. It seems many of us do that. We hear an alarm or receive some warning, and our first thought is to ignore it. Many of us immediately think everything will be okay and that nothing bad will happen to us. That's our default instinct, a psychological defense mechanism. But when it comes to fire alarms and many other warning signals, that instinctual attitude can lead to big trouble.

One basic lesson is don't be that person who ignores alarms. Fight through your instincts, get up, and get out. This same tendency can also be at work in our spiritual lives. It is so easy for us to get wrapped up in our stressful, exciting, busy, and even purposeful lives and become oblivious to the spiritual alarms going off all around us. Amid so many things we think we need to do or want to do, we can be blind to the one thing we truly need. John Wesley calls it "the recovery of the image of God." That's what we need: an inward transformation from arrogance to humility, from self-centeredness to living in love for God and all of God's creation.

In our spiritual lives, we can get stuck in a fantasy world

107

believing that everything is okay, believing that we are free when, in fact, we are imprisoned by the likes of anger and greed and envy, believing we are at peace even "as the pit of hell opens its mouth to swallow us up," to use an image from Wesley. The alarm is going off, and we often don't hear it.

Religion can be an obstacle. When John Wesley was preaching, England was in the midst of a great change. It was the beginning of the Industrial Revolution. The world was changing from an agricultural focus to an industrial focus, from rural to urban. People were flocking into cities, and the cities did not have the infrastructure or government processes to handle it. The pressing issues included poverty, disease, education, unsafe working conditions, child labor, sanitation, hunger, drugs and alcohol. Charles Dickens, writing at the same time, called this "the best of times, the worst of times." And what was the attitude of the church? Well, since the church was primarily for those whose lives were more stable, to put it nicely, the people of the church tended to retreat, to lock themselves inside for nice, comfortable Bible studies and teas. Wesley drew upon an image that Jesus used to describe this: the image of a painted tomb, beautiful on the outside, all nice and clean, but full of dead bones on the inside.

The whole Methodist movement started as John Wesley and others took one hard step, and that step was from inside the church to outside. Wesley was awakened. He looked around, and God called him, and many others, to do something. So, these first Methodists started methodically setting up systems and processes to make a difference. Here's one example. In a time when education was only for the elite, the Methodists believed that everyone deserved an education, so they set up schools. And since so many of the children they were trying to reach had to work six days a week, the only option left was Sunday. So, guess what these schools came to be called? Sunday School. It is the forerunner to our commitment to education for all. That's one example of how our predecessors changed the world.

In the scripture, the Apostle Paul says we were once in darkness. We were lost. Wesley gives a long list to describe this condition: lost in profaneness, slandering, Sabbath-breaking, gluttony, drunkenness, revenge, injustice, extortion, fraud, lies, self-centered egotism, the conditions, he says, that "spread over our land like a flood." Once, we were in this darkness, but, as Paul says and Wesley echoes, "Now in the Lord you are light." Notice this: Paul says we are called to do more than shine a light. He says, "We are light." We illuminate "all that is good and right and true." That's the description of those who are awake in the Lord.

Sisters and brothers, it is time for us to wake up. The great trumpet of the Lord is blowing, calling us to life, calling us to peace and joy in the Holy Spirit, to holiness and happiness, indeed to heaven begun on earth. That's at the heart of true religion. In the third sermon in Wesley's Standard Sermons, the inspiration for this chapter, it is clear that true religion is not rooted in anything "external to the heart" or outside of a personal relationship with God. Doctrines, creeds, and our church buildings are all important. They are God-given resources for us to grow in faith, but they are not the focus. God wants us all to come to know God's love inside. That's what God wants for us. That's what turns on the light,

109

empowering us to shine with love, peace, and joy in a world that needs these life-giving blessings.

In Wesley's sermon, he uses the parable of the Prodigal Son as inspiration (Luke 15:11-32). In the midst of a very hard time, this son "came to himself." He remembered home. He remembered he was loved. As we look more closely, we see that this is an initial awakening, with more to come. It is like when our eyes first open after sleeping. It takes a while to see clearly. In this moment, the son develops a plan to say, "Father I have sinned against heaven and before you; I am no longer worthy to be called your son; treat me like one of your hired hands." His plan was conceived out of deep guilt and shame. But then we read, "While he was still far off, his father saw him and was filled with compassion and ran to him and put his arms around him and kissed him." It is a graphic description of grace. It is in this reception that he truly "came to himself." In this act of grace, he could begin to see more clearly who he was through the eyes of his father.

That's the kind of love we can all know when we "come to ourselves" when we "wake up." Deep inside, this truth dwells in you. Deep inside, this truth is calling for you. To all who need to hear this word, in whatever way you need to hear it, "Sleeper awake! Rise from the dead, and Christ will shine on you" and through you.

Amen.

Reflections for Personal Devotion and Discipling

1. Have you ever felt like you're physically awake yet asleep as you go through the motions of life or faith?

When we think about being asleep, we often think about our eyes being closed as we're in a restful, reclining position. When Wesley calls his listeners to wake up, he's not talking about waking up from physical sleep. Instead, he calls for people to wake up from "a deep sleep of the soul." We find ourselves in this place when we forget that we are made in the image of God. Have you ever felt like you're physically awake yet asleep as you go through the motions of life or faith? You may not have your eyes closed, but your soul is crying out, "What must I do to be saved?" or, in other words, to live a life that has been awakened by the transforming love and light of God?

2. Do you need to be awakened right now? If not now, when have you been awakened from spiritual sleep?

We may have all experienced moments when we realize we've been asleep too long. We've let our faith fall to the wayside or tried to tackle the world on our own and then realized that we have been spiritually asleep all this time. The story of the prodigal son (Luke 15:11-32) provides us with a picture of what it looks like to be awakened from "a deep sleep of the soul." After journeying away from his father, trying to make it on his own, the prodigal son is awakened and returns home to his father, who is excited to welcome him back! In the same way, God welcomes us when we awaken. God responds in grace when we seek to experience the light of Christ that surrounds us and resides in us. Thinking about the prodigal son's story, do you need to be awakened right now? If not now, what has awakened you during a time in your life when you were spiritually asleep?

3. What is good about the words "retreat," "sanctuary," and "refuge"? What are the potential dangers, spiritually speaking?

Often, churches emphasize the importance of retreats, silence, and resting in God. We think self-care is an important part of being a spiritually well-rounded person. Yet, during Wesley's time, he was concerned that the church was viewed—perhaps too much—as a place to retreat from the world's problems. While these words like "sanctuary" and "retreat" have merit, what are the potential dangers, spiritually speaking?

CHAPTER TEN

"Scriptural Christianity"
(A devotional paraphrase)

Sermon 4 in The Standard Sermons of John Wesley

"All of them were filled with the Holy Spirit."

Acts 2:4

Paraphrase of Wesley sermon

When Pentecost came, they were all in one place. And suddenly, there came a sound from heaven like a rushing, mighty wind. And there appeared to them tongues as of fire. And they were all filled with the Holy Spirit, and all began to speak to others in ways they could understand and hear of the wonderful works of God through Jesus Christ. This great event sparked the birth of the Church.

That story is found in Acts 2. In Acts 4, we hear a similar story. The disciples had been praying and praising God, and again, they were all filled with the Holy Spirit. In these great events, there is no mention of other extraordinary gifts of the Spirit, such as speaking in unknown tongues. Even in the early church, God gave these extraordinary manifestations of the Spirit with a sparing hand. As Paul asked, were all prophets? Had all the gifts of healing? Did all speak in tongues? Perhaps not one in a thousand. So here is

113

the point: they were all filled with the Holy Spirit for a much greater purpose than these works.

When the Holy Spirit comes, all disciples are given the one thing essential in all ages, and that is "the indwelling of Christ and the holy fruits of the Spirit—love, joy, peace, patience, kindness, gentleness, goodness, faithfulness, and temperance (Gal 5:22-24). By the Spirit, an inward transformation comes so outwardly we can walk with Christ in "the work of faith, in the patience of hope, and in the labor of love" (1 Thess 1:3). That is the heart of our faith—not a set of opinions, not a system of doctrine, not the manifestation of extraordinary powers, not speculation about the future or what abilities are required. All these concerns can distract us from what is truly important. At the core of our faith is a change that happens in hearts and lives, beginning in individuals and spreading from one to another.

Imagine one person being touched to the heart by the Apostle Peter preaching at Pentecost. Imagine this one being convicted of sin, repenting, and believing in Jesus. How does the scripture describe this personal event? It is being able to say, even in an initial way, "Christ now lives in me and the life which I now live, I live by faith in the Son of God, who loves me and gave himself for me" (Gal 2:20; see also Rom 8:15-15, 1 Cor 12:3). In this relationship is peace, the peace that passes all human understanding. In this peace, we are no longer afraid to live or die, for we now live in a love stronger than the power of death (Phil 1:23). In Christ, we are a part of something bigger than ourselves and able to live from an eternal perspective. We are able to say, "Behold what manner of love the Father has given unto us that we should be called children of God" (1 John 3:1).

Secondly, this love always comes to us on its way to someone else. If we try to hoard it or keep it to ourselves, it will grow as stale as old bread. This love grows as it is shared. "We love because God first loved us" (1 John 4:19). The great miracle is how this love opens our soul to every other soul, even those we might deem as "evil" or "enemies." As our hearts are pierced and God's love gets in, we begin to see all souls as those for whom Christ died. In the mystery of faith, we even pray for them and give them a special place in our hearts. That's what the Spirit does.

Imagine even a few who know this love and what they might do as they see the world's true condition before them. How could they not be moved by the many sights of misery? Would they not pour their hearts into the work of "plucking some of these brands out of the burning?" Would they spare no pains to bring back to the Great Shepherd "poor sheep that had gone astray" (1 Pet 2:25)? Would they not labor "to do good to all before them" (Gal 6:10)?

At the heart of true Christianity is nothing other than love. This is what spreads from one soul to another. This is God's design for the church, not to indoctrinate or create systems for "us" against "them," not to come together for comfortable conversation and fellowship with no challenge that might pierce the heart even more. That is not the kind of holiness to which we are called. Our calling is to the holiness of love, love that is not "puffed up," that does not insist on its own way, that is patient and kind, gentle, and temperate in all things, always seeking what is good for the other (see 1 Cor 13:4-8). This love saves us from passion and arrogance, lust and vanity, and every temper that is not in Christ. This love is at the heart of scriptural Christianity. This love grows into the world through us—from one soul to another.

This may sound sweet and nice, warm and fuzzy, like this talk of love. But make no mistake, as the early Christian movement grew, so did the offenses. Many were moved even to persecute the movement. In both government and religion, those in power were especially greatly offended. Their worldview and places of privilege were being challenged. The disciples were "turning the world upside down" (Act 17:6). But as the pillars of hell were shaken, the kingdom of God spread more and more. Sinners everywhere turned from darkness to light.

To grow in this love, we must be "watered of God," to use an old phrase. This nourishment and cultivation—this "watering"—happens in community. It happens as we attend to the ordinances of God, the ordinary channels of God's grace, and the methods of Methodism: in "the Apostle's doctrine," in "receiving that food of the soul with all readiness of heart through worship and the reading of scriptures," in "the breaking of bread," and in the prayers and praises offered up by the congregation. This is how we grow in grace, increase in strength and in the knowledge and love of God.

So, let us see the vision of the prophets of old where swords are beaten into plowshares and spears into pruning hooks, where nation shall not rise up against nation and war shall be no more. Imagine the earth, full of the knowledge of the Lord (Is 11:6-9). That's the vision of what is before us, a vision of the very kingdom of God. As this kingdom "gets inside," it transforms us from one degree of glory to another (2 Cor 3:18). We begin to imagine peace where no harm comes to our neighbors and no oppression "grinds the face of the poor." We begin to live in God's eternal love as revealed in Christ our Lord. This is the vision at the heart of true and scriptural Christianity.

Now, let me speak plainly. Does this kind of Christianity exist here and now? Are we among those filled with the Holy Spirit and bearing the true fruits of the Holy Spirit? Do we let other theological matters distract us from this core purpose? Who among us is willing to work for a continual revival of this Spirit? Are you willing to count your fortune, liberty, and life to be an instrument of this work?

Lord, take us out of the mire that we not sink! May the Holy Spirit come—to me, to you, to others through us, filling us all with the love that is truly at the heart of all faith. Keep us from distractions. Keep us attuned to the gospel. Keep our hearts in Christ Jesus our Lord.

Amen.

"More Than...Extraordinary"

Acts 2:1-6

How was your day? Imagine someone saying, "Oh, it was nothing special, pretty ordinary." Or you prepare a big meal and then ask someone if they enjoyed it, and they say, "I would describe it as ordinary." We often associate "ordinary" with boring, mundane, nothing special. But in matters of faith, "ordinary" is worthy of our attention.

When Wesley first explored this word, he was dealing with people looking for God in the extraordinary. People were looking for God in great signs and wonders, burning bushes and prophetic dreams. People wanted answers written in the sky.

Wesley reminds us that these extraordinary "manifestations of the Spirit" are given sparingly. Extraordinary gifts only come to a few and only at special times. On the other hand, ordinary gifts of the Spirit are for *all*, and they bind us together rather than set us apart. Look at what the Apostle Paul says about this. He asks, "Were all prophets?" No. "Do all have the gift of healing?" No. "Does everyone speak in tongues" (1 Cor 12:29-31)? No. Wesley says, "Maybe not even one in a thousand." So, perhaps we need to focus more on the ordinary, everyday ways the Holy Spirit moves in our lives.

Maybe we need to focus more on the one thing God wants for everyone every day. And what is that one thing? It is Christ in our hearts where we are able to live our ordinary lives knowing we are loved, and in Christ, we can grow in the fruits of the Spirit: love, joy, peace, patience, kindness, goodness, generosity, faithfulness, and temperance/balance/ self-control (Gal 5:22-23). With these common blessings at work among us, we can "walk with Christ in the work of faith, in the patience of hope, and in the labor of love" (1 Thess 1:3). This is how God works through us in our everyday, ordinary lives.

Reflecting on my ordinary week, I can think of a couple of times when I saw God at work. This week, I sat in a hospital room with a family gathered around a husband, father, and grandfather who had recently entered hospice care. There were no miracle healings. There were no extraordinary signs. But during our gathering, God's eternal grace flowed through tears and even laughter as stories were told. God's peace, the peace beyond our ability to explain, was there. It was a holy moment.

Also from my ordinary life, I met a mother and daughter in the church parking lot one Wednesday night as they were wondering which door to enter. People were going in all directions—to children's choirs, to "The Well" for dinner, to youth and mid-youth. As I asked if I could help them, two of our mid-youth came running out to meet them. They had invited their friend to come to the mid-youth choir. They took her away as quickly as they had arrived, and what I noticed was the smile on the mother's face. It was such an ordinary thing for seventh-grade girls to do, but I promise you, I saw Christ in that ordinary moment.

Earlier, we reviewed the story of Pentecost, when the Holy Spirit came upon the church in a mighty way. We might easily get hung up on the big event and lose sight of the purpose. Yes, on this day, the disciples were given the power to speak other languages, but the bigger miracle was that others heard the good news. The Spirit moved in their lives, and, by the Spirit, many came to know, deep inside, the One who gave his life for them and opened up the way of life for all. They came to know the One whose love for us is stronger than death itself. And then they all received a common calling, the true test of the Spirit's work in our lives. They wanted to share this good news with others.

This calling to share God's love is a big part of our vision statement at the church I serve. We say, "God's love comes to us on its way to someone else." If we try to hoard this love or keep it to ourselves, it will grow as stale as old bread. This love only grows as it is shared. In our everyday lives, the Holy Spirit is at work, empowering us to speak words that will help others hear God and act in ways that help others come to know God's love. That's the ordinary, common calling of the Holy Spirit upon all disciples. This movement started at Pentecost.

In a *TED Talk*, scientist Suzanne Simard spoke about how trees communicate with one another.[15] Before this discovery, it was thought that trees competed against one another for water and light, but instead, they send messages back and forth through an elaborate underground network to balance resources, share information about dangerous diseases, and support one another. In this vast network, trees aren't seeking extraordinary gifts to outdo one another; instead, they use the gifts given to cultivate a healthy community.

Could this amazing tree network be a parable for us?

I think of what the Apostle Paul says when he cries out, "I beg you to live a life worthy of the calling to which you have been called, with all humility, gentleness, and patience, bearing one another in love, eager to maintain the unity of the Spirit in the bond of peace" (Eph 4:1-3). This is the ordinary, everyday work of the Spirit in our lives. We might miss this work when looking for some extraordinary sign. If we are too focused on the extraordinary, we are likely to get off track in our spiritual lives. We are likely to hunger and thirst for power rather than for the blessings of God. We are likely to retreat into modes of self-protection rather than give ourselves to the self-sacrificing love of Christ. That is not what God wants for us. And so, we must intentionally focus each day on the ordinary, everyday gifts God gives.

If you read the paraphrases of Wesley's sermons, you'll note that he tends to end his sermons with questions that call us to self-examination. I want to do the same. Are you growing in the ordinary fruits of the Spirit, the fruits given to bind us together and create healthy relationships and community? Are you open to God's love as it comes to you on its way to someone else? Are you attentive to what Wesley calls the "ordinary channels of God's grace," such as weekly worship, daily prayer, reading the scriptures, and the God-given resources that keep us growing in our ability to listen and follow? May the common gifts of the Spirit and the ordinary fruit of the Spirit become a regular, everyday part of your life.

Amen.

Reflections for Personal Devotion and Discipling

1. Why do we come together for worship? How does worshiping in community help us stay strong in our faith?

Wesley often emphasizes that the means of grace—scripture, prayer, worship, and others—are not the end goal but resources to help us seek and experience God's love. We cannot be steadfast in our faith if we don't have resources and people keeping us accountable. Why do we come together for worship? How does worshiping in community help us to stay strong in our faith? The nourishment and growth that happens in our lives is sustained when we receive communion, pray, or hear the scripture read among other believers. What is meaningful and life-giving about worshiping in community with others?

2. How does love become powerful? Why might some perceive love as dangerous?

Christianity grew throughout the early church because people loved one another, and this love spread from one person to another. As the love between people was passed from one to another, people in the early church began to be persecuted by those in power, by both the government and the religious leaders who were offended and afraid their power and privilege were being challenged. This radical, powerful love was perceived as dangerous. How does love speak to power? Why might some perceive love as dangerous?

3. How would you define the words "ordinary" and "extraordinary"?

We often think of the ordinary as boring or unexciting and the extraordinary as special and exciting. We hear stories of God communicating with people in extraordinary ways through burning bushes and dreams, and we acknowledge these experiences never happen to us. Or we hear of people being given extraordinary gifts like speaking in tongues or healing or interpreting dreams, and we think of ourselves as ordinary and unlikely to receive such exciting gifts. Yet, when we think of the ordinary and extraordinary in this way, we have it all backwards! Extraordinary gifts are only given to a few people. But ordinary gifts are given to all people. We have all received the fruits of the Spirit. Without these fruits, extraordinary displays can be harmful and divisive.

4. Throughout this exploration of Wesley's sermons, we will see the fruits of the Spirit listed repeatedly. It was a constant theme for Wesley. What are these fruits? What virtues can we add to the list using other passages and sources?

We invite you to take some time this week to memorize Galatians 5:22-23 and reflect on the ordinary gifts of the Spirit you have received as one who is loved by God.

CHAPTER ELEVEN

"Justification by Faith"

(A devotional paraphrase)

Sermon 5 in The Standard Sermons of John Wesley

*"For there is no distinction, since all have sinned
and fall short of the glory of God; they are now
justified by his grace as a gift, through the
redemption that is in Christ Jesus."*

Romans 3:23-24

Paraphrase of Wesley sermon

We were created in the image of God to reflect God's
own love. And, according to the creation story meant to
illuminate our lives, God gave one prohibition: "Thou shall
not eat of the tree that is in the middle of the garden." This
tree was a sign that God's love is not forced. We are free to
live in God's grace and share in God's work of cultivating
and creating. This tree symbolizes our freedom. And what
happened? Well, we (not just "they" but "we") disobeyed God.
We ate of the tree and suddenly noticed we were naked—
exposed, vulnerable, and fearful. We had fallen. Death
entered our minds, our hearts, and our world.

This story is the backdrop for the doctrine of
justification, our theme for the day. "Justification" is an

important theological word for understanding who we are in our relationship with God. The Apostle Paul explains it this way: by the sin of the first Adam, who represents us all, we all fell short of the life and love of God. Instead of freedom, we found ourselves bound by greed, envy, anger, and lust. We became immobilized by fear, focused on self-protection and building ourselves up. We traded the truth for a lie. And over it all, we hung the cloud of death, the great cause of our deep fear. This human condition sparks the need for some remedy and hope.

So, what does it mean to be justified? Getting technical, justification is not being "made just" and "good." The theological term for that is "sanctification." We will get to that, but for now, we can say that sanctification is the fruit of justification. They go together, but they are distinct gifts. Justification implies what God does FOR us through Christ; sanctification describes what God works IN us by the Holy Spirit, transforming us into those who are able, once again, to reflect God's love and live by the virtues of true holiness— patience, kindness, temperance, and others—that illuminate the very character of God.

In scripture, justification is pardon or forgiveness rooted in compassion and God's ability to see what is happening deep within. The opposite is condemnation and imprisonment. It is also a legal term describing acquittal or "wiping the slate clean." In scripture, this word is used to show that "all have sinned and fall short of the glory of God" and thus "are now justified by his grace through the redemption that is in Christ Jesus" (Rom 3:24). And later in the same letter, we read: "Therefore, since we have been justified through faith, we have peace with God through our Lord Jesus Christ ... through whom we have gained access by faith to this grace in which we now stand" (Rom 5:1).

The next question before us is this: Who are those justified? The answer goes against our conventional wisdom and shows how God's ways differ from those of the world. We assume it is the innocent who go free. We also assume the guilty need to make amends before they (we) are set free. This is even argued in scripture, with James affirming that we are justified by works and not faith alone. Many, even today, from parents to teachers to bosses, proclaim that we must be sanctified—that is, good—before we can be justified—set free, advanced, or welcomed to the table. Conventional wisdom calls for restitution and good works before such blessings are given. In other words, it is to be earned.

We proclaim something very different from the dominant perspective in the scriptures and at the core of our doctrine as a church. Who does God justify? The answer is clear. God justifies the "ungodly" (Rom 4:5). Jesus came to "seek and to save the lost." He uses the image of a physician who comes for the sick, not those who are healthy. Christ comes to those "in whom no good dwells, who are full of envy, anger, and love of the world—all the genuine fruits of that 'carnal mind' which are the enemy of God." He looks upon the heart and knows what is possible for us as those created in the image of God. Through Christ—the second Adam—God responds first with mercy.

So, how do we come to receive this gift? How do we come to know this gift and live by its blessings? The answer is faith. From a deeply theological and biblical definition, faith is a divine, supernatural conviction given by God (Heb 11:1). Faith is a deep trust in the heart that God was in Christ reconciling the world to himself and not counting our sins against us" (2 Cor 5:19). It is a divinely given, deeply personal trust and confidence that Christ not only dies for the sins of the whole world but also for *me*. God loves *me*, gave himself for *me*, and opens up to *me* the way of life and love.

Apart from this love, we are lost in the fear of living and the dread of death. We are "aliens from the commonwealth of Israel and without God in the world" (Eph 2:11f). The very moment God gives faith—and it is a gift of God—faith is "counted as righteousness." We are welcomed into relationship with God, and the way of life is opened up to us. We are restored to a "right" relationship and "are no longer strangers and aliens but are citizens with the saints and members of the household of God." That's justification.

It may sound strange that God would receive us so easily that the condition would not include some work by us, some attempt to prove ourselves worthy. We were created to live in God's love, but we can't do this until this love is in us. God first loves us; then we can love (1 John 4:19). This gift comes before we *do* anything. To try and justify ourselves is to bring God down to our level and try to make God conform to our understanding and conditions for love. Our efforts only dim the light to the glory to which we are called.

So, as we are led to this recognition that we can't save ourselves, that's when we are able to turn to the One who has the power to take away the sin of the world. Don't try to justify yourself or claim good works. Don't try to be humble, contrite, or sincere as cause for God to bless you. Plead only the blood (the life) that was given for you and to you. The ransom paid for your proud, stubborn, sinful soul. Plead only for mercy. Come quickly! Put your faith in the Lord Jesus Christ, who reveals this gift and reconciles us to God.

Amen.

"More Than...Being Good"

Luke 18:9-14 and Romans 3:21-26

Two men went to the temple to pray. One of them was a religious leader. He was comfortable standing before the altar. He "stood and prayed thus with himself." Note these words: "with himself," about himself, perhaps even to himself. "God, I thank you that I am not like others, especially not like that guy over there." This part of the story reminds me of afternoon talk shows where people expose their problems for the whole world to see, and we watch and say, "Wow, at least my life is not *that* bad."

This religious leader then tells God (and himself) all he does. And to be honest, it is an impressive list. "I fast twice a week," he says. As another religious leader, I'll tell you this is a good practice. I recommend fasting, and so does Jesus. "I tithe," he says. Once again, that's good. This practice helps us live for something more than what we have and enables us to bring God's blessings into the world. Before we are too hard on this Pharisee, I can find many passages in the Bible that tell us to do what he does. So, what's the issue?

Let's look at the other guy in the temple for a moment. He is a tax collector, which, in that day, means he was the lowest of the low. Today, we would not compare this man to the IRS but to the Mob. Back then, tax collectors could collect anything they wanted as long as they paid what the King demanded, and they did so with the power of the Roman army behind them. In today's world, we might imagine a drug dealer, perhaps, who ruined the life of someone you love but with full legal protection. This man had the nerve to come before God and ask for something. He asks for mercy. Do you think God will answer that prayer? Would you? Would you be willing to show mercy?

Here we have two persons. One is a good, moral, Bible-believing, generous person who went home empty. The other is an immoral, thieving mobster who went home blessed. It is the sinner who goes home justified. How can that be "justified?" Here's the key to the parable. Jesus says, "For those who exalt themselves will be humbled, but those who humble themselves will be exalted."

Think about a wheel. With a wheel, strength, power, and inspiration come from the center, the core, the hub. What is at the center of your life? If you put yourself at the center, you cannot move very far. On our own, we are "poor in spirit," says Jesus. We are humble, whether we know it or not. We do not have the spiritual resources within ourselves to make life meaningful and certainly not to connect life to eternity. We can't do that. On the other hand, if we put God at the center, we are exalted. We are then connected to a source of true power and can move forward in grace, mercy, and love—all that God wants for us.

The Apostle Paul says it this way: we all fall short of the glory of God. If we think our goodness is the standard, we bring God down to our level and make it a standard that is easy to meet. From this perspective, we don't have very far to go. Just fast, tithe, walk around looking religious, throw in some judgment of others, and you've got it made.

If, on the other hand, we allow the Spirit to open our eyes to the glory of God and the magnitude of God's love, then we truly see just how big God's love is and how short we fall. We know there is no way we can make it on our own. Our hope, if there is any hope at all, is in the very love that the Spirit has revealed to us.

Paul says that even as we fall short, we are also justified by grace through the redemption in Christ Jesus. Justification is a technical and legal term meaning "acquittal" or "pardon." Justification is when a judge "wipes the slate clean." From another perspective, we can think of lines on a page and justified margins. To justify is to align or bring together, creating balance, order, and meaning. We fall short. We "miss the mark." We can't bring ourselves in alignment with God's hope for us. Christ Jesus does this FOR us on the cross, opening up the way of life with pure and perfect love. And in this restored and aligned relationship, we are able to grow in all the fruits of the Spirit, the fruits of sanctification, "with all humility, patience, and gentleness, bearing one another in love" (Eph 4:1-3), as Paul says. This is the method by which salvation is given.

So, who receives this? Who is justified? We often assume the guilty must make amends before being set free. Conventional wisdom calls for restitution before grace is given. In other words, grace needs to be earned by things like fasting, tithing, and looking religious, with a good dose of judging others, and then salvation is earned. That's the perspective of our conventional wisdom. God's perspective is very different. Justification (pardon, forgiveness, alignment, restoration) comes to those who know the need for mercy. Justification is made known as we begin to understand the depths of God's love and as we begin to trust in this blessing.

God plants this love in our hearts, and we respond with faith and trust. We begin to let this love rule and guide us.

I was in a conversation one day with a college student who was wondering how God could be both a God of justice and mercy. Through this conversation, we explored the thought that mercy is how God brings justice. Mercy is not saying, "Oh, it's okay. You're forgiven. I don't expect anything from you." No. Mercy is an invitation to change. It is an invitation to embrace the love you are given and to start living by that same love. In this sense, mercy can be painful. It calls us to be transformed, to live by a new standard. It is worth noting that the Hebrew word for "mercy" is akin to the word for "womb." Mercy is the place where new life is born. Yes, God forgives and pardons, showing great mercy while calling us into new life to grow into all we are created to be. That's the way God works.

The Pharisee did not ask for anything from God and thus went home empty. The known sinner asked for everything; he asked for God's mercy. He asked for Christ and went home full, a changed man. May this story lead you to examine your own heart.

Amen.

Reflections for Personal Devotion and Discipling

1. How might this distinction between the different kinds of grace help us understand the different ways God works in our lives, in others' lives, and in the world?

An important and foundational doctrine in the Wesleyan tradition is grace. A basic understanding is that grace is the gift of God's steadfast and eternal love. Yet, as we look at grace more fully, we discover there are many layers to this doctrine. First is prevenient grace, known as the grace that comes before. This grace is present in us before we even know who God is. Then there is justifying grace, or justification, and after this is sanctifying grace, or sanctification. In this sermon, Wesley offers an extremely helpful distinction between justification and sanctification. Justification is "what God does for us" through Christ, while sanctification is "what God works in us" by the Spirit. How might this distinction between the different kinds of grace help us understand the different ways God works in our lives, in others' lives, and in the world?

2. Who is justified by God? Why would God justify the unholy, ungodly person rather than those who are already holy? What does this idea of justification say about who God is?

In the world, it is common to believe that a person should be holy before they receive justification or forgiveness of sins. By the ways of the world, we tend to assume that restitution must be made before a pardon is given. Yet, if a person is already reconciled with God and their sins have been forgiven, why must they be justified? As Wesley says, "To assert this is to say the Lamb of God takes away only those sins which were taken away before." Wesley wants to be clear that God comes to justify the unholy, the sinner, the imperfect one. He gives examples to help us understand this point, including the shepherd who comes to find the lost sheep rather than the sheep that had not strayed or the doctor who comes to heal the sick, not the healthy. God does not require that we become holy first but, instead, offers us love and grace through Jesus without judging who we have been. What does the perspective reveal about the character of God? What are the implications for us?

3. If faith is rooted in a gift from God rather than something we develop and possess on our own, how might we think about faith differently?

Grace comes first. It is a gift to us. Our hearts are opened to this blessing, and then we are able to respond in faith. First, God loves us; then, we are able to trust in this love. Wesley defines this faith as "a sure trust and confidence that Christ died for 'my' sins, that he loved 'me,' and gave himself for 'me.'" Grace gives us this inkling within that God is for us. Faith is our response. We give our lives to this love, as revealed in Jesus Christ, with the Holy Spirit as our guide.

CHAPTER TWELVE

"Righteousness of Faith"

(A devotional paraphrase)

Sermon 6 in The Standard Sermons of John Wesley

"For Christ is the end of the law so that there may be righteousness for everyone who believes."

Romans 10:1-13

Paraphrase of Wesley sermon

What does it mean to be righteous? For a basic definition, to be righteous is to stand in a right relationship with God or to be in covenant with God. The term also points to certain virtues and values believed to be "right." Beyond this, the answer requires deep and careful reflection. Misunderstanding this grand theological term can create a huge stumbling block to our growth in faith and to the joy God wants for us. There are two big understandings of righteousness within scripture, and their relationship is complex. On the one hand, we have righteousness based on obedience to the Law of God. On the other hand, we have righteousness through faith.

God's first covenant, given to us through the Hebrew people, was based on law. Obedience was the standard for acceptance and inclusion in this covenant. In the biblical narrative, when humanity lived fully in God's grace, fulfilling this covenant was possible. But after "The Fall," this became impossible. Even today, this kind of devotion to God remains impossible for all "conceived and born in sin." And yet, this understanding of the covenant remains, that righteousness, or right relationship, with God depends on our obedience.

This standard of obedience is easily corrupted. In our natural state and by the ways of the world, we are compelled to build ourselves up, prove ourselves before others, and claim our own goodness, often by putting others down. Scripture says that this way of relationship is rooted in sin. Even, or maybe especially, in religion, we pour on these expectations: "Stand fast in faith," "Give in thanksgiving," "Be sincere in prayer," and "Do not live as others do." Maybe by throwing in some judgment of others, righteousness is revealed. In our desire to be religious, we put all this on ourselves. We want to show God what we can do. We turn religion into rules and policies, standards of behavior and etiquette, making religion manageable and enforceable from our perspective. We turn religion into a system rather than a relationship.

How many of us have fallen into the temptation to "establish our own righteousness in order to be accepted by God?" We work to prove ourselves, and in doing so, we bring God down to our level. In the process of justifying ourselves, we lose sight of God's true glory and grace. This great stumbling block must be removed.

If the law is our judge, there is no room for failure or flaw. If this is the standard for our acceptance and inclusion in God's covenant, we are in trouble. If we only focused on a few "thou shall nots," some might make it, but even then, most would have to rely on many offerings and confessions. Once we factor in the "thou shalls," we see how short we fall. At the heart of these positive commandments is the call to love God with our whole being and to love every soul as God loves them. We see this even in the Hebrew scriptures. Even thinking about things contrary to this love is sin. With this standard, who could possibly stand and claim righteousness and worthiness before God?

A new perspective on righteousness—actually, a very old perspective—removes this stumbling block made new in our lives. In the first book of the Bible, we hear of Abraham becoming the father of Israel and how his offspring would be like the stars of heaven and would be blessed as lights to the world. We are then told that Abraham believed in this promise, and it was credited to him as righteousness (Gen 15:6). At this point, a different standard for righteousness was given and took on new life in the coming of Christ our Lord. From this perspective, faith stands in the place of obedience. We come into right relationship with God not by proving to God how good we are but by trusting in God's true goodness—God's unmerited love and pardoning mercy. This way of righteousness magnifies God rather than bringing God down to our level.

Strictly speaking, in this new covenant, we do not have to *do* anything. There are no requirements of works or knowledge. From our perspective, we enter this covenant simply by trusting in what God has done and will do, as revealed in Jesus Christ. This is what is meant by the phrase, "Believe in the Lord Jesus Christ, and you shall be saved." Faith is coming to trust in the love that God has planted in our hearts. Faith is giving ourselves to this love as we come to know the love that God has already given through Jesus Christ. In this way, faith is first a gift to us and then a response from us. It brings us into a right relationship with God or, in other words, into salvation.

To compare side by side, the first covenant supposes that we are already holy and worthy. The second supposes that those included in this covenant are unholy, know they have fallen short of the glorious image of God, are first bound to sin and death, and yet trust in God's righteousness as revealed in God's forgiveness, mercy, grace, and deep love for us as well as God's desire to transform us.

So, practically speaking, how do we submit to the "righteousness which is of God by faith." The first step is to disclaim our own righteousness. We look in the mirror and face our self-will, foolish desires, and vile affections. We admit that we are lovers of pleasure more than lovers of God. We deserve nothing from God but indignation and death. At this point, we face the truth and stop trying to live the self-justifying lie.

That's when the light breaks forth and reveals the true righteousness of God, not as a judge but as pure love. Therefore, whoever you are, as one who desires to be reconciled to a good, forgiving, gracious, and merciful God, do not say in your heart, "I must first do this. I must first conquer my sin. I must first go to church, hear more sermons, or be more sincere in my prayers." With these thoughts, you are trying to establish your own righteousness as the ground of your reconciliation. First, only believe. Believe in the Lord Jesus Christ. It is not about being contrite enough, or saying the right words, or confessing the right steps. Simply trust in God's love as the Spirit opens the way. Know the truth. Righteousness comes through faith. Oh, sinner, believe in the One who says, "I will be merciful to you, and your sins I will remember no more" (Heb 8:12).

Amen.

"More Than...Obedience"

Romans 10:1-13

As Pastor Lauren and I discussed how we might illuminate this word from Wesley, we were trying to think of biblical stories, and one that came to mind was the story on the Tower of Babel in Genesis 11. It is meant to be a funny story, even as it hits with a profound truth. This story is a second ending to the story of Noah. After the flood, Noah and his descendants were charged with being fruitful and multiplying and filling the earth, but in this story, we are told that they tried to do things differently. They worked hard to build a city to "contain themselves," it says, and to keep themselves from being scattered into the world.

In this Tower of Babel story, we are told the people started building their city with bricks and tar instead of stone and mortar. This is an important clue. Almost every Hebrew hearing this story would have laughed at this point. Back then, bricks were nothing more than baked mud, and tar would not hold the bricks together for long. This group of people, says the story, "wanted to make a name for themselves." So, they decided to build a mighty tower that would reach all the way to heaven. As they gaze upon this "great accomplishment," we are told that the Lord had to "come down" to see it. It is a wonderful satire. In the end, God pushes them out of the nest, so to speak, and scatters them, thus nudging them to fulfill their purpose. These people had to step out in faith and learn to rely on a power much greater than their own.

A few chapters later, we come to Abraham's encounter with God. God tells him to pack up and head out "to a land that I will show you." In other words, Abraham and Sarah are not told where they are going. They were invited to step out in trust. The scriptures tell us that Abraham and Sarah trusted God, and this trust was declared as righteousness.

"Righteousness" is a keyword for us today. At its root, it simply means a "right relationship with God" or "in covenant with God," where we are called and empowered to live by certain God-given virtues and values. In the scriptures, we have two big understandings of righteousness. We see both of these views in both testaments. On the one hand, we have righteousness based on obedience to the law. On the other hand, we have righteousness rooted in faith. Distinguishing between them continues to be a struggle for us, for there is some truth in both.

It is easy for us to believe that our righteousness, or being right with God, is based on what we do. And, I must say, we preachers can feed this idea. We say it all the time: "Stand fast in faith," "Go to church," "Give your tithes and offerings," "Be good." And it might be easy to get the impression that this is the way into God's good graces, that we are supposed to build our way up into God's presence, that it is up to us to "make a name for ourselves" and "prove ourselves to God" like the people gathered around the Tower of Mud.

But here's the problem with this understanding of righteousness. If our acceptance is based on us being good, then it is only natural that we will make our list manageable. We will naturally bring God down to our level.

We will make the requirements easy for us to meet. "Go to church when it is convenient." "Put something in the offering plate." "See religion as keeping things stable and comfortable for those on the inside, maybe throw in some judgment of those outside so you can justify not associating with 'those people,'" and then we've got it made. We set it up to make a "name for ourselves before God."

But then God "comes down" into our neat little religious order and turns on the light. Suddenly, our eyes are opened. We start to see just how far we have fallen short of the true glory of God. In this light, we begin to see the true magnitude of God's love for all creation, and we know there is no way we can live up to this love on our own. Our only hope, if there is any hope at all, is in the very love that God "comes down" to reveal.

In this light, we begin to understand that a right relationship with God cannot be based on us proving to God how good we are but only by trusting in how good God is. The Apostle Paul calls it "righteousness by faith." Faith! Is it not something we must do to be saved or to live in a right relationship with God? Here's where understanding this doctrine is so important to our spiritual health. Faith is putting our trust in God, but before we can do this, we must have something in which to trust. God's love comes first. God opens our hearts to know that we are not alone, that we are loved, and that God is there to see us through, even through death itself.

God gives cause for faith, and then we can give our lives to this relationship and then believe. And get this. Not believing does not lead immediately to judgment or condemnation—not from a God who abounds in steadfast love. As we wrestle with matters of faith, God does not pile on judgment but rather meets us with compassion and grace. God first wants us to know that we are loved. This love is our salvation. That's what is meant when we are told in our lesson that "the word of God—the blessing of God's love—is near." It is on our lips and in our hearts. It is right there, and it is for everyone to receive.

So, if you desire to be reconciled to God in "right relationship," do not say in your heart, "I must first do this. I must first go to church, hear more sermons, or be more sincere in my prayers." No. Such attempts can become huge stumbling blocks to a right relationship with God. With these thoughts, you are trying to "establish your own righteousness" rather than trust in God's righteousness for you. First, only believe. Believe in the Lord Jesus Christ, who is God's love given to us. Here is the question for you today: Is God's Spirit communicating with your spirit that you are loved and a child of God? Do you know this in your heart, in that place deep within where words fail to express fully? If so, then respond by believing and giving yourself into this relationship. God is working in your life for the promise is sure: "Everyone who calls on the name of the Lord shall be saved."

Amen.

Reflections for Personal Devotion and Discipling

1. Why might approaching our relationship with God through the lens of the righteousness of law be problematic? What does it say about our perception of who God is? What does it say about God's relationship with humanity?

   Wesley distinguishes between "righteousness of the law" and "righteousness of faith." When we live by righteousness of the law, we have a mindset of "do this and live." In other words, what we do in this life is what earns us salvation. Why might this way of approaching faith and God be problematic? What does it say about our perception of who God is? What does it say about our relationship with God?

2. How is our understanding of God and God's relationship with humanity different than above when viewed through the lens of righteousness of faith?

   When we live by righteousness of faith, we have the mindset of "believe and live." The law requires us to be obedient and perfect in all things, whereas righteousness of faith invites us to first believe in who God is and what God does for us through Jesus. How might approaching God and God's relationship with humanity be different through the lens of righteousness of faith?

3. How does declaring our sinfulness set us free?

   When we subscribe to the idea of righteousness of law, we require ourselves to act with "unsinning obedience." But when we subscribe to the righteousness of faith, we declare that we are sinners but that God's love overcomes our sinfulness. Wesley says it this way in his sermon, "Thou art sin! God is love! Thou by sin are fallen short of the glory of God; yet there is mercy with him." By faith, we are given a freedom that transforms us, not because we seek to be perfectly obedient but because we attest to our sinful nature and open ourselves to God's work in us and through us.

CHAPTER THIRTEEN

"The Way of the Kingdom"
(A devotional paraphrase)

Sermon 7 in The Standard Sermons of John Wesley

"The kingdom of God is at hand;
repent and believe in the gospel."

Mark 1:15

Paraphrase of Wesley sermon

"The kingdom of God is at hand; repent and believe in the gospel." These words point to true religion, described by our Lord as "the kingdom of God." These words also point the way to this kingdom, "Repent and believe."

We start with the nature of true religion, or the kingdom of God. The Apostle Paul uses this same term and says, "The Kingdom of God is not meat or drink, but righteousness and peace and joy in the Holy Spirit" (Rom 14:17). True religion is not "meat or drink." Paul said this because many within the young church were demanding that certain rules and rituals be followed, especially those that revolved around the dietary laws of the Holiness Code. It was the big issue of the day. Should we, or should we not, follow the rules about clean and unclean foods? Many were saying the law must be kept in order to be saved (Acts 15:1, 24; 21:20). Laws around

147

circumcision were also prevalent. It was believed that Gentiles must submit in this way if they wanted to be a part of true religion.

The Apostle Paul boldly proclaimed that true religion is not found in any law external to the heart. The whole substance of true religion is found through relationship with the One who brings righteousness, peace, and joy in the Holy Spirit. While certain rules and practices may be helpful and even appointed by God as good, they are not the substance of true religion. All rituals and rules are means to a larger end. If they take over our hearts and become ends in themselves, they become an abomination to the Lord. Let no one dream they are more, even those rules and ways that seem so dear to us.

True religion does not consist in orthodoxy or right opinions. A person may be orthodox and a zealous defender of doctrine. This person may think rightly concerning the Trinity, the Incarnation, and every other doctrine and creed we uphold but still have no religion. Such a person may be as orthodox as the devil, knowing that Jesus is God's son but not following him and subverting his message.

This alone is true religion: righteousness, peace, and joy in the Holy Spirit. First, righteousness. We cannot misunderstand this term if we stay focused on the two great commandments on which "hang all the law and the prophets," namely, love of God and love of neighbor as a part of yourself. The first great commandment is to love God with all our heart, soul, mind, and strength. To love God is to delight in serving God and growing in God's love. In this love, the heart's desire is to glorify—illuminate, magnify—

ADVENT, CHRISTMAS AND EPIPHANY

God in all that we do and say. The second commandment is to love your neighbor as a part of yourself. It is to embrace others with the most tender goodwill and seek for them every possible good. Within these callings are planted the virtues that lead to the fruit of righteousness in the world: humility, kindness, gentleness, and patience.

True religion, or a heart right towards God and humanity, also implies happiness and holiness. It is not only righteousness but also "peace and joy in the Holy Spirit." This peace from God banishes all fear, the fear that torments the soul, the fear of the misery that surrounds us in the finite world, and the great fear of death. This is the peace that passes all human understanding. The joy that comes is more than mere happiness. This joy is a deep happiness that rejoices in the assurance that we are reconciled to God through Jesus Christ and called beloved children of God.

Holiness and happiness joined into one! That's the kingdom of God. Whenever the gospel of Christ is shared, God's kingdom comes. It is right before us. And at first sight, we see that it is less about what God wants *from* us and more about what God wants *for* us.

And so, we hear the voice cry out, "Repent and believe in the gospel." Repentance is the call to "know yourself," to look inside and see that you are a sinner, corrupt in every way. In this corruption, our passions and desires are "out of frame," distorted, and disorienting. In this corruption, we might say deep in our heart, "Who is the Lord that I should serve him? Let him serve me, if anything." This corruption breeds a love for independence, pride, greed, and thinking that we have all the answers. From this evil fountain flows the bitter streams of vanity, thirst for praise, covetousness, and lust of the eye. From this fountain boils up anger, hatred, malice, revenge, and envy, along with the fruits of contention, gluttony, drunkenness, luxury, vain sensuality, and adultery. If not prevented, we are likely to drown in everlasting misery.

And so, we are called to repent, to recognize and turn. The call comes with much urgency. Repent! And then believe. Believe in the gospel. The gospel is good news for all guilty, helpless sinners. It is the word we use to connote the whole revelation of God made through Jesus Christ. At its core is this: Jesus Christ came into the world to save sinners. Or, to put it another way, "God so loved the world that he gave his only Son, to the end that we might not perish, but have (even right now) everlasting life" (John 3:16).

Believe this, and you will be walking in the kingdom of God. Your sins are forgiven. Righteousness, peace, and joy surround you.

Only beware that you do not deceive your soul and think this faith is just an assent to the truth of the Bible or the articles of our creed. Even devils believe *that* God exists and *that* Jesus is God's son. The faith to which we are called is so much more. This faith is a sure trust in the mercy of God through Christ Jesus our Lord. It is a confidence in a pardoning God. It is a divine conviction that God was in Christ reconciling the world to Godself and not counting our sins against us. It is believing *in* God and trusting God's presence and guidance.

Do you believe? If so, then the peace of God is in your heart, and sorrow and sighing are fleeing away.

Do you believe? If so, your soul magnifies the Lord, and your spirit rejoices in God, your Savior. You rejoice in the hope of eternity. Do you believe? Then, the love of God now fills your heart. You love God because God first loved you. God's love comes to you on its way to another. Being filled with love, peace, and joy, we are also filled with patience, gentleness, faithfulness, goodness, humility, temperance, and all the other fruits of the same Spirit. These fruits reflect the very image of Christ, and we can grow in this image, from one degree of glory to another (Gal 5:22-23, 2 Cor 3:17-18).

According to Mark's Gospel, it is the first thing Jesus says. He looked out upon so many weighed down by religion and the so-called wisdom of the world, and he said, "The kingdom of God is at hand. Repent. Right before you, turn and find the blessings of forgiveness, love, righteousness, peace, and joy. Trust in this good news. It will change everything. Everything!

Amen.

More Than...Religion

Romans 14:13-20 and Mark 1:14-20

Jesus came proclaiming that the kin-dom is at hand. This kin-dom is big! To describe it can be a daunting task. There is almost no way we can wrap our little, finite human minds around it without help from above. Perhaps think of explaining quantum physics to a three-year-old, and we might begin to understand the problem. Since this was the main topic of Jesus' teachings, he had to find a way to help us "get it." And he did so less with lectures or formulas and more with stories. We call them parables.

The kin-dom of God, for example, is like a mustard seed. It is the smallest of seeds and grows into the greatest of shrubs. Okay. Everyone in that culture would have known this. Yes, it is a mystery, a tiny seed growing into a bush. It is an inspiring lesson but nothing extraordinary or out of place. But then Jesus adds a twist, as he does with many parables. Jesus says that this seed becomes a tree where all the birds of the air can come and nest in its branches. Now, that's something new. In the kin-dom, a seed—a life—can be transformed into something completely new. And where on earth will we see birds of many different species nesting together in the same tree, making it a common home? That doesn't happen here, but it is what the kin-dom of God is like.

So often, when we hear this term, we think of something "out-there," something beyond this world, a place reserved for us when we die. Yet, Jesus says that this kin-dom is at hand. It is in our hearts, and it changes everything.

You may notice the use of the term "kin-dom," without the "g." Both "kin-dom" and "kingdom" are translations. Many use this different translation to illuminate what Jesus intends and move away from an old understanding of human organization. This new translation suggests kinship and relationship, with God working not only "over" all but also in and through all to bring love to life. While there is a place for both translations (and we are using both), the emphasis on "kin" moves us away from a hierarchical, patriarchal image and perhaps closer to what Jesus is trying to communicate. The kingdom, or kin-dom, he illuminates greatly differs from our typical human ways of organizing ourselves.

Here's another parable from Jesus. The kin-dom of heaven may be compared to someone who sowed good seeds in a field, but while everybody was asleep, an enemy came and sowed weeds among the wheat. The workers in the field want to know if they should pull up the weeds. The landowner says, "No." Let them grow together until the harvest, for in gathering the weeds, you might uproot some wheat as well. "At harvest time," said the landowner, "I'll sort it all out, collecting the weeds and bundling them to be burned and gathering the wheat into my barn."

In the natural way of things, that's just not how it is done. So, to "get it," we must change our perspective and allow God to transform our hearts so we can live from a whole new orientation. The kin-dom of God is about transformation. And in God's fields, it is even possible for weeds to be transformed into wheat. Weeds, representing what is going on in our heart, can be transformed. We get to work on that as we live and grow in the "fields" of our daily lives. By the grace of God, selfish pride can be transformed into humility. Hatred, envy, and malice can become love for all. That's what happens as God lives in and among us. And at harvest time, when it all gets sorted out and the weeds in our heart are separated from the wheat in our heart, may we all still be able to recognize ourselves after this sorting happens. What will be left in you?

In our first scripture lesson, Romans 14:13-20, we hear about people in the early church demanding that certain rules and rituals be followed, especially those revolving around the dietary laws of the Hebrew people. It was the big issue of the day. Should we, or should we not, follow the rules about clean and unclean foods? For many at that time, "true religion," or representing God's kin-dom on earth, was wrapped up in all these outward rules and rituals. God's rule was defined by rituals, creeds, and many "dos and don'ts." So, echoing Jesus, Paul proclaims that the kin-dom of God is not rooted in any law, creed, or even scripture, or anything outside the heart. All these things are important resources, but only as they lead us to God found within.

The kin-dom of God is not meat or drink (or in anything external to the heart). The kin-dom of God is justice, peace, and joy in the Holy Spirit. In this kin-dom, love rules, and we are able to grow in the fruits of this love—humility, kindness, gentleness, and patience. Paul says the kin-dom of God is peace, the peace that can overcome all the fears that might torment our souls, the fears of truly living, the fears of dying, and "this time" being all there is. God comes to calm these fears.

Next, the kin-dom of God is joy. This joy is much

more than mere happiness. Happiness depends on the circumstances around us. If things are going well, then we can be happy. There are also a lot of times in life when we are unhappy. But even in these moments, we can know joy, for joy is a gift of the Spirit, springing up from deep within where the circumstances of the world have no power. Joy is a deep, abiding assurance that we are loved and that nothing in life or death can separate us from this love. Having this gift planted deep within, we can rejoice (have joy) in all circumstances. Yes, the kin-dom of God is not rooted in anything external to the heart or any outward circumstance, as we learn in scripture and through the teachings of Wesley. The kin-dom of God is peace, joy, and eternal love planted within.

What can we do to discover these blessings? The first step is to look inside. Turn towards the spiritual mirror and face who you are and what is happening inside. We could give elaborate definitions of "repentance" and "believing," as we have before, but at the heart of it is a willingness to let God transform you from within. When this happens in us, everything changes.

What is the kin-dom of God like? Well, it may be like a person who is angry, even with God, and then something moves them deep inside to come to church, and they feel that anger melt into forgiveness, understanding, and even joy.

What is the kin-dom of God like? It may be like a person struggling with addiction who is given the power to overcome and, by grace, begin a new life.

What is the kin-dom of God like? It may be like looking in the mirror and seeing eyes full of envy and lust and a heart full of selfish pride and greed and then, in that same spiritual mirror, seeing the possibility of love, peace, and joy and wanting that more than anything.

What is the kin-dom of God like...for you?

Amen.

Reflections for Personal Devotion and Discipling

1. What are the pitfalls or dangers of considering religion as creeds and practices? How does thinking about religion in this way lead to divisions and judgment? What are the advantages of thinking of religion as an inward experience that takes place within the heart?

In this sermon, Wesley clearly defines "true religion." He first states that it is synonymous with "the kingdom of God." He then says true religion is not about creeds, laws, or any rituals, "nor indeed in any outward thing whatever; in anything exterior to the heart." Instead, true religion is found in righteousness, peace, and joy in the Holy Spirit. Wesley repeatedly tries to make it clear that when we put doctrines, rules, and rituals at the heart of religion and use them to judge and divide, we become witnesses of something false and not of God. These resources are blessings and also a means, but they are never the end, or purpose, of life-giving faith.

2. How has your idea of the kin-dom of God transformed as you think of it as a place that is here, now, within you, not a far-off place? How does the translation of "kin-dom" open up new perspectives?

At the beginning of this section on "More Than," we discussed that salvation is about more than entry into heaven. Salvation also happens in the here and now. This same idea is true for the kin-dom of God. We often think of the kin-dom of God as synonymous with heaven, a place far away in both time and space, a place we will get to one day. But as Wesley illuminates the kin-dom of God, it is as "heaven opened in the soul." Review the parables that illuminate what Jesus means when he uses the term. Review the explanation for using both translations, "kingdom" and "kin-dom." What are the images provoked by each term?

3. In Romans 14:17, Paul lists righteousness, peace, and joy as synonymous with the kin-dom of God. Reflect on how these gifts of righteousness, peace, and joy lead to true religion.

Read Romans 14:17. Wesley uses this verse as the basis for his definition of the kin-dom of God. He explains what is important about each of these characteristics throughout this sermon. Righteousness describes a "right relationship" with God, which comes through faith in what Christ has done for us, not because of anything we have done. As Wesleyans, we take this a step further than many. This right/aligned/justified relationship with God leads to righteous living in relationship with others. The Great Commandment to love God and love neighbor is our guide. The next blessing is "peace," according to this verse. This peace banishes fear, fear of God's wrath and condemnation and of death. The next characteristic is "joy." This joy is deep, true happiness. Joy flows from our souls because of who we are in God. How do these gifts of righteousness, peace, and joy change our lives and bring life to the world?

CHAPTER FOURTEEN

"The First Fruits of the Spirit"

(A devotional paraphrase)

Sermon 8 in The Standard Sermons of John Wesley

*"There is therefore now no condemnation
for those who are in Christ Jesus."*

Romans 8:1

Paraphrase of Wesley sermon

No condemnation exists for those who live by grace as a part of the Body of Christ (Rom 8:1). This is such good news, yet frequently misunderstood. This knowledge of grace can create a lazy attitude about our relationship with God as if it doesn't matter what we do because God is gracious anyway. To counter this delusion, we must ask, "What does life in Christ look like?" And in this context, ask, "What does it mean to say there is no condemnation for those who live by grace?"

To be in Christ means to be joined in the Lord by God's grace, not by our own righteousness. This grace, however, is much more than a legal judgment of forgiveness or a gift of inclusion without any worries about how we live. That understanding is a delusion. As the scripture says, being in Christ is "to walk in the Spirit" rather than "walk in the flesh." In Paul's writings, the word "flesh" signifies our corrupt nature (see Gal 5:16-19). Those who are in Christ have "crucified the flesh with its affections and lusts." They live by a vision that calls them to abstain from all the works of the flesh—from idolatry, hatred, strife, envy—from every word and work that flows from the corruption of God's intent. With every fresh assault on those in Christ, there is also a fresh occasion to praise and cry out, "Thanks be to God who gives us victory through Christ Jesus our Lord."

To be in Christ is to walk by the Spirit in heart and life and to grow in the fruits of the Spirit—love, joy, peace, patience, kindness, gentleness, faithfulness, humility, temperance—and whatever else is worthy of praise (Gal 5:22-23, Phil 4:8). Those who walk in the Spirit cultivate this fruit daily and do all things to the glory of God. On this journey, we are transformed by the Spirit, from one degree to another, in the ways of love, the "well of water springing up to eternal life" (2 Cor 3:18, John 4:14).

That's what it means to be "in Christ" and to "walk by the Spirit." There is no semblance of grace being cheap or leading to lazy faith. The free grace of God comes as a high and holy calling to become all that God created us to be.

And here is good news. As we make this journey, there is no condemnation. This is the second point we want to explore. At the first level, there is no condemnation for past sins. It is as if all past sins were stones thrown into the deepest sea. To be in Christ is to be free from all guilt. In Christ, the peace of God is ruling in our heart, flowing from a continual sense of God's pardoning mercy. The chains have been lifted; bondage is no more; we are free.

But what if a follower of Christ loses sight of this mercy and strays into darkness? My answer is this: to not stand in the mercy of God is to not believe. Faith implies light. To lose the light is to lose faith. This happens, even to true believers. It is possible to lose the light of faith and fall again into bondage for a time, but this does not mean that God abandons us. When we are "in Christ" and believe in his name, there is no condemnation. As we walk in the Spirit of grace and mercy, we are not lost, even amid great trials and temptations. The light shines in the darkness, and the darkness cannot overcome it (John 1:5).

Likewise, there is no condemnation from any present sin or inward sin. If the seed of God's love remains, we cannot sin or be separated from God. The seeds of pride, vanity, anger, and lust may still be present, especially in those who are "babes in Christ," but they are not subject to the law. Although they may feel the evil nature within them and hearts of deceitfulness, if they do not yield or shut themselves off to the mercy of God and remain in continual war with all sin, there is no condemnation. God is well pleased with our continuous, sincere-though-imperfect obedience and desire to be transformed.

Although they are continually convicted of sin, although they know they do not love God with all their being, although they feel self-will mixing with their best desires, although wandering thoughts still come as they pour out their hearts to God, still there is no condemnation. As we walk by the Spirit, the acknowledgment of these manifold defects only gives them a deeper sense of the love of God, and this becomes, even more, the desire of their hearts. This acknowledgment and continual spiritual work empowers growth in love. This is the fruit that comes on this journey "in Christ."

Lastly, there is no condemnation for anything whatsoever that is not in their power to help, whether it be of an inward or outward nature. For example, if the Lord's Supper is to be administered in worship and you cannot participate because of sickness, there should be no guilt. God's mercy and understanding rest over our frail natures. A believer may sometimes be grieved because they cannot do what the soul longs to do. One may cry out if detained from worshiping. But in this omission, God is not displeased in any way.

If there is no condemnation for those who walk in the Spirit, why be fearful? Even if one sins again and the heart is moved to repent, that faith, once again, cancels all that is past, and there is no condemnation. From every moment you trust in Christ, all sins vanish as the morning dew and "life and peace" come. As the Apostle Paul says, we are set free in Christ, and we did not receive this freedom to fall back into fear and bondage (Rom 8:1-14).

At the same time, this good news does not diminish the fact that to sin is to stray from the life-giving way. Do not deceive yourself. Do not say "peace" when there is no peace. Do not fall into the trap of trying to justify yourself. It is good to face what is happening inside you and submit yourself to the transforming grace of God. As you walk in the Spirit, pour out your heart to God. Cry out as one in need of healing. Pray for strength to fall no more. Trust in God to heal your backsliding and to fill you again with the faith that works by love.

On this journey, Christ is our guide. We can rely on him. As we walk in the Spirit, we will be transformed into his likeness from one degree of glory to another. Wait in peace for that hour when you are fully transformed and, in that moment, able to recognize yourself and give thanks for all the graceful growth that came along the way.

Amen.

"More Than...Fearful Faith"

Mark 2:13-17 and Romans 8:1-6

Jesus is walking along the beach. Did you catch that? Jesus and his disciples are "beside the sea," and a big crowd has gathered around him. Walking along the beach, Jesus saw a man named Levi sitting at his tax booth. Does that not sound a little strange? It might be easy for us to picture a lemonade stand or maybe a booth where someone is selling vacation packages or renting snorkeling gear, but a tax booth at the beach is a little strange. I can see it now. A parent says, "Hey, kids, let's go to the beach this afternoon. We can swim, eat, listen to a man named Jesus for a while, and pay our taxes at the conveniently located tax booth."

At the fair last year, there was a group giving away Bibles and engaging people in conversation. Out of curiosity, I stopped and watched this booth for a while, noticing that people would see this possibility up ahead and start making decisions. Some went straight to the booth for more free stuff. Most people, however, would walk as far to the other side as possible and work hard to avoid eye contact.

I suspect that Levi was getting that kind of response. Tax collectors in that day were not very popular. Their job was to collect funds for the occupying government, and they were free to add large service charges to the bill, all with the backing of the Roman Army. So, I doubt many were freely going to Levi's tax booth. The scripture says Levi was just "sitting at the tax booth." And then, something happened. Jesus noticed him. Jesus approached him. Jesus invited him to come along as he and his disciples walked along the beach. And Levi gets up and leaves his booth behind.

Now we must read between the lines. My guess is Levi had been listening for a while. I suspect he had heard Jesus speak about how much God loves us. Perhaps Levi had overheard stories from the crowd of how Jesus touched people and healed them and how he forgave sins. Jesus took the initiative and included people like him. This was something new. Could it really be true? So, when Jesus noticed him and invited him to come along, Levi's heart was ready.

I love this story because of the way it illustrates the gospel. Our relationship with God starts with an unconditional, undeserved, unmerited act of love. As Paul says in Romans 8:1, "In Christ, there is no condemnation." To use an image from Wesley's sermon on this theme, it is as if all our sins are stones thrown into the deepest sea. This is the first blessing or "first fruit" that comes to us from God. God first loves us before we do anything, regardless of anything we have done.

It is important to note the religious leaders' reaction to this outpouring of love. They are incensed that Jesus would welcome sinners and tax collectors in this way. Good religious leaders simply should not set that example. But that's who Jesus is. Jesus comes as the one who reveals God to us, precisely for all who need this pure and perfect love.

Now, we need to be clear about what this love is and is not. This love we are given is not a naïve or easily manipulated love that might lead to a lazy attitude about our relationship with God, believing that it doesn't matter what

165

we do because God will love us anyway. God will indeed love us no matter what, but this does not mean God doesn't care what we do or turns a blind eye to how we live. You may have heard the saying, "Love is blind." I get that at one level, but I prefer this saying: "Love is not blind; it is the only way we can truly see."

Here's the way Paul characterizes it in our second scripture lesson. God's love reveals two paths before us; we see the way of the flesh on the one hand and the way of the Spirit on the other. The way of the flesh signifies our sinful nature. It is not to say that our bodies are bad. God loves this part of us. God calls the body a temple, a place where God wants to dwell. When we walk along the path of the world apart from the Spirit, we find ourselves surrounded by weeds of greed, envy, anger, lust, and selfish pride. On this path, fear is everywhere. In fear, we focus on getting and securing, winning and earning our way, and ensuring no one knows what is happening deep inside. And then we fear, perhaps most of all, that "this" is all there is.

In God's love, this way of the flesh is exposed. God helps us to see it, but always in the light of a new possibility, the way of the Spirit. The first blessing (or fruit) of the Spirit is knowing we are loved, and nothing we do or don't do can ever separate us from this love. In this love, the words of Jesus come to life: "Do not be afraid." All our human shortcomings and wayward ways are met with forgiveness and grace. The way of the Spirit is revealed, and we are invited just as we are to come along and grow in all the fruits of the Spirit that truly reveal the way of God: love, joy, and peace. Along this way, we learn how to be patient and kind.

We are able to practice gentleness and temperance. Jesus invites us to come along with him on this journey.

Perhaps you have felt like Levi must have felt that day. Have you ever felt trapped in a cycle that was anything but life-giving, just "sitting in your booth," so to speak, perhaps pouring your energy into finding ways to block the fear? Turn on the TV. Eat more. Pour a drink. Take a pill. Find some way to push back the pain. And then the Spirit of God nudges you and invites you to something greater. Maybe that is happening in your heart right now. You glimpse being a part of something bigger than yourself and your needs. You want more. Something moves you to get up and turn to the vision of true life that God is opening up before you. Like Levi, you decide to follow Jesus.

Jesus wants more for us than a life of fear and flesh, as if this were all there is. The Spirit of Christ comes to us in our heart and says, "Walk with me." How do you respond?

Amen.

Reflections for Personal Devotion and Discipling

1. What blessings come to us with the "first fruits of the Spirit?" How is grace often misunderstood? How does God's love lead us to love others more fully?

   The first fruits of the Spirit can be summed up in the word "grace." The word "grace" simply means "gift." Our journey in Christ starts with this undeserved, unmerited gift. With this gift, we can truly heed the words of Jesus, "Do not be afraid." In Christ, there is no need to fear, even as we struggle and fall along the way.

2. Continuing the thought above, how does the "first fruit" of knowing we are loved motivate growth in the fruits of the Spirit? How does the gift of forgiveness and grace lead us into a life of discipleship?

   Wesley's words might be compared to a popular distinction by Dietrich Bonhoeffer. In his book, The Cost of Discipleship, Bonhoeffer distinguishes between "cheap grace" and "costly grace."[16] To paraphrase, he says that cheap grace is forgiveness without repentance, baptism without growing in the means of grace, and communion without confession. Cheap grace is grace without discipleship, grace without the cross, grace without Jesus Christ. On the other hand, true grace is costly because it calls us to follow, and it is grace because it calls us to follow Jesus Christ. It is costly because it costs a man his life, and it is grace because it gives us the only true life. It is costly because it condemns sin, and it is grace because it justifies the sinner. Above all, it is grace because God "did not reckon his Son too dear a price to pay for our life, but delivered him up for us." How does this distinction help us understand Wesley's call to grace? How might we live into costly grace? What resources does the church provide?

3. How does it feel to hear that there is no condemnation for any past or present sin? How does this good news change us?

Paul describes the gospel in many ways. In our lesson this week, he says there is "no condemnation for those who are in Christ," no condemnation for any past or present, inward or outward sin. This does not mean that sin is gone, but it lets us know how Christ works for us as we face our sin and open ourselves to God's transforming love.

4. What does it mean to "walk in the Spirit," and how does this differ from "walking in the flesh?"

As the paraphrase reveals, the term "flesh" signifies our nature apart from the spirit. It is not that "flesh" is bad. In fact, our material nature is loved by God. This nature is redeemed by the Spirit and becomes life-giving in relationship with God. In Christ, we are able to "walk in the Spirit" and, with our whole being, grow in the fruits of the Spirit. We are called to cultivate this fruit daily. How does this distinction help us become all God has created us to be?

5. Concluding this series, why did Wesley start his Standard Sermons with these eight themes? How do they set the tone? What does it mean to say that these sermons are doctrine for us?

Review the themes and ponder how they are foundational for our growth in faith. What is important about the order of these themes?

About the Authors

Michael Roberts is the senior pastor at First United Methodist Church in Jonesboro, Arkansas, and previously served at First United Methodist Church in Conway, Arkansas, where this book began to take shape. He holds degrees from the University of Central Arkansas (B.A.), Duke University Divinity School (M.Div.), and Southern Methodist University (D.Min.). He has served on the Cabinet as the Director of the Restart Initiative and as the Director of Connected In Christ, an intentional leadership and congregational development process designed to "facilitate the connections needed for faithful and fruitful ministry." He also serves on the General Conference delegation for the Arkansas Conference. His wife, Dede, is also an ordained United Methodist pastor, and they have three children, all adults, and two grandchildren.

Lauren DeLano Grosskopf is the associate pastor at First United Methodist Church in Russellville, Arkansas, and previously served as the pastor at Vilonia United Methodist Church and with Michael Roberts at First United Methodist Church in Conway, Arkansas. She holds degrees from Hendrix College (B.A.) and Boston School of Theology, Boston University (M.Div.). She also serves on the Jurisdictional Conference delegation. Her husband, Dr. Jacob Grosskopf, is an associate professor of geology at Arkansas Tech University.

Endnotes

1 The reordering of Wesley's sermons to fit within the liturgical year is unique to this series and is offered as a way to bring these teachings to life in a new way. As we went through the year, we developed a worship series for Lent building upon Wesley's sermons: "The Wilderness State," "Manifold Temptation," "Self-Denial," and "Original Sin," among others. We developed a series for Easter that built upon the sermons "New Birth," "Marks of a New Birth," and "The Great Privilege of Those Who are Born of God," and then led up to Pentecost with "The Lord Our Righteousness," "The Witness of the Spirit," "The Witness of Our Own Spirit," and "The Spirit of Bondage and Adoption." During Ordinary Time, or the season after Pentecost, we explored the core teachings of Jesus using Wesley's thirteen discourses on the Sermon on the Mount. This was followed by a series on Discipleship, Stewardship, and Spiritual Growth, building upon multiple sermons including "On Schism," "A Caution Against Bigotry," "Catholic Spirit," "Sin in Believers," "Cure for Evil Speaking," "Use of Money," "The More Excellent Way," and "Christian Perfection."

2 Thomas A. Langford, *Practical Divinity: Theology in the Wesleyan Tradition* (Abingdon Press, 1983), 25. The scriptures convey the knowledge of God "as its words are transposed to experience by the Holy Spirit." These sermons as doctrine are meant to facilitate this movement.

3 Paul Wesley Chilcote, *Multiplying Love: A Vision of United Methodist Life Together* (Abingdon Press, 2023) p.60 and Paul W. Chilcote, *Recapturing the Wesley's Vision: An Introduction to the Faith of John and Charles Wesley* (IVP Academic, 2009) P. 27. "Faith is a means to love's end...Faith without activated love (on the one hand) and works founded upon anything other than God's grace (on the other hand) are equally deficient visions of the Christian life."

4 Howard A. Snyder, *The Radical Wesley, The Patterns and Practices of a Movement Maker* (Seedbed, 2014) Kindle location 845. He says, "Wesley was very clear that salvation was wholly by grace alone. But he was equally insistent that God graciously enabled men and women to cooperate with the Holy Spirit in the great work of salvation, of restoring the image of God."

5 Ted A. Campbell, *Methodist Doctrine: The Essentials, 2nd ed.* (Abingdon Press, 2012), 59f. Wesley wanted to illuminate the "process by which women and men actually live out the life of grace." This is referred to as the "way of salvation." As "first order theology," Wesley's sermons illuminate this way.

6 Ashley Boggan Dreff, "The Wesley's Enduring Message" United Methodist Communications, August 2022 (a podcast with transcript).

"John and Charles Wesley were God-loving agitators and Spirit-filled dissidents. They knew how to find a line, walk right up to that line and then jump right over it." Here Dr. Boggan Dreff explores the history of "consenting to be more vile" in Bristol, following George Whitfield's lead. After being criticized and threatened for move, Wesley defended himself and other preachers with the phrase, "The world is my parish." In this context, the world is not seen as the globe but as one step outside of the church.

In this important lecture, Dr. Boggan Dreff uses the coined word "vile-tality" to explore ways in which we might reclaim our calling to spread the love of God to as many people as possible. Wesley consented to be "more vile" in his decision to proclaim the gospel outside the walls of the church and meet people where they were, using language that would be relevant and understandable. This was a major turning point for the movement. And it doesn't end with him. For another example, Mary Fletcher Bosanquet, as one of the first female preachers within the movement, said: "I am conscious how ridiculous I must appear in the eyes of many ... I do nothing but what Mr. Wesley approves, and as to the reproach thrown by some on me, what have I to do with it, but quietly go forward saying, 'I will still be more vile, if my Lord requires it.'" "It's four o'clock somewhere." If you know, you know.

7   For examples of this teaching, see the video series "A Graceful Way – Methodist History and Doctrine," YouTube @michaelroberts3091. There are 12 videos, published during the pandemic, including "Wesley Who?," "Epworth to Aldersgate," "The Birth of a Church," "True Religion," "Scriptural Holiness," "Wesley and Calvin," "The Way of Salvation," and "The Via Media," Michael Roberts, 2021.

8   Lauren Winner, *Wearing God* (Harper One, 2015), 102.

9   I have written some on this topic with a little more depth. See "Authority of Scripture, a Wesleyan Hermeneutic, and the Way Forward," at connectedinchrist.net, Dec. 2018, Michael Roberts. For more, see "Wesley on Human Sexuality (and his commentary on often cited verses)," connectedinchrist.net, July 2022.

10 This idea of a "fourth gift" has been the theme of many sermons. In addition to Wesley's sermon, I was inspired by David Bartlett and Barbara Brown Taylor, *Feasting on the Word: Year A, Volume 1: Preaching the Revised Common Lectionary* (Westminster/John Knox Press, 2010), 217. Also, Thomas Troeger, "The Magi's Fourth Gift," Biblical Preaching Journal, Winter 1997.

11 See Thomas Langford, *Practical Divinity: Theology in the Wesleyan Tradition* (Abingdon Press, 1983).

12 Michka Assayas, "From Bono: In Conversation with Michka Assayas," ©2005 by Michka Assayas. Found in *Christianity Today* at www.christianitytoday.com, 2005.

13 Michael Roberts, "Salvation is More than a Decision, It's Biblical," Arkansas Conference, 2001.

14 Kenda Creasy Dean, *Almost Christian: What the Faith of Our Teenagers Is Telling the American Church*, (Oxford University Press, 2010), 12, 71-74.

15 Suzanne Simard, "How Trees Talk To Each Other," TED Talk, July 2018.

16 Dietrich Bonhoeffer, *The Cost of Discipleship* (SCM Press, 2011), 45f. Originally published in 1937.

Made in the USA
Columbia, SC
16 November 2024

46705750R00100